The Bottom Line

Your Career in Accounting

Ronald J. Thacker, Ph.D., CPA
Professor of Accounting
University of New Orleans

M. Frank Barton, Ph.D., CPA
Assistant Professor of Accounting
Memphis State University

Special Contributors:

P. Merle Maddocks

Beauregard J. Parent, Jr.
Tulane University

Thomas Horton and Daughters, Inc.
22 Appleton Place / Box 3 / Glen Ridge, New Jersey 07028

Material from the Certificate in Management Accounting Examinations, Copyright ©1974 by the National Association of Accountants, is reprinted with permission.

Copyright ©1977 Thomas Horton and Company
All rights reserved
No part of this work covered by copyright hereon may be reproduced or used in any form or by any means—graphic, electronic or mechanical, and photocopying, recording, taping, or information storage or retrieval systems—without written permission of the publisher.

ISBN 0-913878-14-6
Library of Congress Card Number 77-92047

Editing and Typography by
Spencer Graphics and Editorial Services, P.O. Box 21068,
Cottonwood, Utah 84121

Printed by R. R. Donnelley & Sons
Crawfordsville, Indiana, U.S.A.

For the Accounting Student

This book has been especially prepared for you—the accounting student. It is a handy reference that you will find indispensable as you move along in the exciting field of accounting.

Let us now tell you a few things about why the book was written and about how you will find it a useful tool.

Why the Book Was Written

For many years now, the field of accounting has grown in an astounding fashion. It is becoming an area with more and more excitement. Accounting is exciting because jobs are available, because careers can be carved out, and because a tremendously important benefit accrues to society from the accounting profession. In fact, the institutions—both public and private—in our economic system could not exist without carefully and creatively produced information to assure success of the key decisions.

We wrote this book to assist students and teachers in finding their way about in some of the vital and changing areas of accounting. We have provided timely information that cannot be found under one cover in any single textbook—or in a single reference of any kind.

What the Book Contains

This book contains information about a multitude of topics. Some of these are

—the jobs that are available in your chosen field, along with current salary information,
—the professional examinations that you will complete, and the licensing of your profession (including a sample CPA exam),
—the literature of accounting for your continued reference (AICPA, FASB, etc.),
—the organizations that you will be associated with,
—the opportunities for future education and development,
—the financial statements that accounting produces.

We gratefully acknowledge the contributions of Lee Primiano and Joseph Greco of Montclair State College, and of Charles J. Weiss of Seton Hall University. We also acknowledge the permission of the Institute of Management Accounting of the National Association of Accountants to use problem materials from past CMA examinations.

The authors have a continuing program to improve this publication—to provide new, up-to-date, relevant data in each succeeding edition. Let us know what else you would like to see included. Let us know how we can improve what is already included—and the publication's usefulness will be improved.

Table of Contents

1 JOBS IN ACCOUNTING 1

   110   The Demand for Accountants 1
       111   History 1
       112   Projections 2
   120   Positions with the Federal Government 3
       121   United States General Accounting Office 3
       122   Internal Revenue Service Agents 4
       123   Federal Bureau of Investigation 5
       124   Department of Defense Audit Agencies 6
       125   Other Federal Agencies 6
   130   Positions with State Government 7
   140   Positions in Teaching 7
       141   High Schools and Vocational Schools 7
       142   Colleges and Universities 8
   150   Positions with National CPA Firms 8
       151   General Information 9
       152   Accounting and Auditing 14
       153   Taxes 15
       154   Management Advisory Services 18
   160   Positions with Local CPA Firms 18
       161   Auditing 19
       162   Tax 19
       163   Management Advisory Service 19
       164   Write-up 19
       165   Professional Development 19
   170   Positions in Industry 20
   180   Minority Groups and Women in Accounting 24
       181   Black Accountants 24
       182   Women Accountants 25
   190   CPA Attorneys 26

Contents   v

2 PROFESSIONAL EXAMINATIONS 27
- 210 Information for CPA Candidates 27
  - 211 State Boards of Accountancy 28
  - 212 Sample CPA Examination Questions and Unofficial Solutions 28
  - 213 How to Prepare to Take the CPA Examination 53
- 220 The Certificate in Management Accounting Exam 54
  - 221 Sample CMA Exam 55
  - 222 Unofficial Solutions 70
  - 223 How to Prepare to Take the CMA Exam 74
- 230 Special Enrollment Exam to Practice before IRS 75
  - 231 Sample Examinations 75
  - 232 How to Prepare to Take the Special Enrollment Examination to Practice before the IRS 76
- 240 Chartered Financial Analysts Examination 77
  - 241 The CFA Candidate Study Program 77
  - 242 The CFA Competency Standards 78
  - 243 The CFA Examination 79
  - 244 The CFA Candidate Study Program—General Topic Outline 83
  - 245 Eligibility Requirements for CPA Candidates 87
  - 246 CFA Candidate Application Procedures and Forms . 88

3 ACCOUNTING LITERATURE 89
- 310 Official Literature in Financial Accounting 89
  - 311 Accounting Research and Terminology Bulletins— AICPA 89
  - 312 Opinions of the APB—AICPA 90
  - 313 Statements of the FASB 91
  - 314 SEC Accounting Series Releases 92
  - 315 CASB Standards 93
- 320 Accounting Research Studies—AICPA 93
- 330 Statements of the APB—AICPA 94
- 340 Auditing Literature 94
  - 341 Statements on Auditing Procedure—AICPA 94
  - 342 Statements on Auditing Standards—AICPA 95
- 350 American Accounting Association Publications 95
- 360 Journals in Accounting 97

	370	Texts and General References	98
		371 General Works	98
		372 Accounting History	99
		373 Financial Accounting Theory	100
		374 Cost and Managerial	101
		375 Tax	101
		376 Auditing	102
		377 Quantitative Methods; Systems; Computers	103
		378 Fund Accounting	104
	380	Ordering Publications	104

4 ACCOUNTING ASSOCIATIONS AND REGULATORY AGENCIES 105

	410	Accounting Associations	105
		411 American Accounting Association (AAA)	105
		412 American Association of Attorney-Certified Public Accountants	105
		413 American Institute of Certified Public Accountants (AICPA)	105
		414 American Society of Woman Accountants (ASWA)	105
		415 American Woman's Society of Certified Public Accountants (AWSCAA)	106
		416 Federal Government Accountants Association (FGAA)	106
		417 National Association of Accountants (NAA)	106
		418 National Association of State Boards of Accountancy (NASBA)	106
		419 National Society of Public Accountants (NSPA)	106
	420	The Financial Accounting Standards Board	106
	430	The Securities and Exchange Commission	107

5 ACCOUNTING EDUCATION 109

	510	Advanced Degrees	109
		511 Master's Programs	109
		512 Doctoral Programs	110
	520	American Accounting Association Programs	111
	530	Professional Development AICPA	112
	540	Professional Schools of Accountancy	120

6 SAMPLE CORPORATION ANNUAL REPORT 121

1
Jobs in Accounting

110 THE DEMAND FOR ACCOUNTANTS

The accountant's important role in society has changed and developed considerably in the 1970s. We will now outline some important considerations in the accountant's job market in past years and set forth some predictions.

111 History

During the last few years there has been considerable economic uncertainty. Because of this uncertainty, students in large numbers have recognized the increasing job opportunities in accounting. The supply of accounting graduates is steadily increasing. Fortunately, the demand is increasing as well. This accelerated demand for accountants has occurred during a period when the demand for graduates in other areas has been curtailed.

The supply of accounting graduates for the period 1969-70 through 1975-76 is shown in Exhibit 1-1.

The market has absorbed this increasing supply of accounting degree graduates, and an expanding demand is continuing.

Exhibit 1-1
Accounting Graduates

	AACSB* Member Schools		Other Schools		
Year	Bachelor's Degrees	Master's Degrees	Bachelor's Degrees	Master's Degrees	Total
1969-70	9,800	1,100	8,900	200	20,000
1970-71	11,700	1,600	9,100	300	22,700
1971-72	13,500	1,800	10,300	400	26,000
1972-73	14,900	2,300	11,400	400	29,000
1973-74	16,800	2,700	14,600	700	34,800
1974-75	20,900	3,400	14,500	900	39,700
1975-76	23,100	4,000	16,500	1,200	44,800

*American Assembly of Collegiate Schools of Business

Source: Daniel L. Sweeney, The Supply of Accounting Graduates and the Demand for Public Accounting Recruits (New York: AICPA, Spring 1976), pp. 7-9.

112 Projections

The supply of accounting degree graduates is expected to continue to increase. The projected supply of graduates is shown in Exhibit 1-2.

Exhibit 1-2
Projected Supply of Accounting Graduates

	AACSB* Member Schools		Other Schools		
Year	Bachelor's Degrees	Master's Degrees	Bachelor's Degrees	Master's Degrees	Total
1976-77	24,600	4,600	18,000	1,500	48,700
1977-78	25,300	5,000	18,900	1,900	51,100
1978-79	25,800	5,700	20,100	2,100	53,700
1979-80	26,100	6,100	21,000	2,300	55,500

*American Assembly of Collegiate Schools of Business

Source: Daniel L. Sweeney, *The Supply of Accounting Graduates and the Demand for Public Accounting Recruits* (New York: AICPA, Spring 1976), pp. 7-9.

The demand for *public accounting* recruits is projected to continue to increase. The ratio of demand for public accounting recruits to total supply of accounting graduates ranged from a high of 39 percent in the year 1972-73 to 29 percent in the year 1975-76.[1] Despite this decrease in the percentage, there has been an increase in the *number* of accountants recruited in public accounting. The projections of the expected supply of accountants and the demand for recruits are shown in Exhibit 1-3.

Exhibit 1-3
Projected Supply of Accounting Graduates and Demand for Public Accounting Recruits

Year	Supply of Graduates	Demand for Recruits	Ratio (%)
1976-77	48,700	14,800	30
1977-78	51,100	16,100	32
1978-79	53,700	17,500	33
1979-80	55,500	18,700	34

Source: Daniel L. Sweeney, *The Supply of Accounting Graduates and the Demand for Public Accounting Recruits* (New York: AICPA, Spring 1976), p. 25.

The public accounting profession is expected to employ more than one-third of the projected supply of accounting graduates. This leaves less than two-thirds of the graduates available to compete for the many positions in industry, government, and in private not-for-profit organizations. Industry and government could probably employ four accountants

---

1. Daniel L. Sweeney, *The Supply of Accounting Graduates and the Demand for Public Accounting Recruits* (New York: AICPA, Spring 1976), p. 25.

for each accountant recruited by public accounting rather than the two for each one now available. The shortage of accountants may possibly be covered by the two-year associate degree graduates and by providing more extensive on-the-job training in some areas.

The increased use of accounting information in business decisions and the changing tax systems (along with the increasing demand for accountants in government) ensure a high demand for accountants in the foreseeable future. The increased complexity of the accountant's job will ensure strong demand for accountants with college degrees. Advanced degrees and training will also be demanded.

120 POSITIONS WITH THE FEDERAL GOVERNMENT

Positions as accountants, auditors, internal auditors, internal revenue agents, financial institutions examiners, and contract auditors represent a part of the positions open to those trained in accounting. The entrance salary for junior accountants and auditors in Federal Civil Service during 1976 ranged from about $8,925 to $11,046 annually. Candidates with superior academic records could expect to receive something near $11,046. Experienced accountants with the federal government earn about $22,000 annually and, with administrative responsibilities, they can expect more.

121 United States General Accounting Office

The United States General Accounting Office (GAO) is in the legislative branch of the federal government and is headed by the Comptroller General of the United States. It is responsible solely to Congress. GAO is charged with examining federal departments and agencies and reporting on the manner in which they discharge their financial, legal, and management responsibilities. In addition to reviewing management performance, GAO also does a variety of other work:

1. *Contract Examinations.* Evaluation of policies and procedures used in negotiating and administrating contracts with private industry, including related internal audit.
2. *Systems Review.* Prescribing the accounting principles and standards used by federal agencies.
3. *Special Congressional Assignments.* Special examinations at the request of congressional committees of activities in the executive branch.

Candidates may qualify for a GS-7 or GS-9 position based solely on their educational attainments, as shown in Exhibit 1-4. The term *GS* refers to a general schedule rating assigned to white-collar employees, at both professional and nonprofessional levels.

Exhibit 1-4
Requirements for Management Auditor, General Accounting Office
(No written examination is required)

GS-7

Four full years of study at a residence school above the high school level, which satisfied requirements for a bachelor's degree in a business administration curriculum, including 6 semester hours or equivalent in accounting *or*

Three years of progressive experience in commerce, industry, or government which involved the application of management principles to administrative problems or processes and demonstrated an understanding of accounting principles

Plus: In addition to one or the other of the requirements stated above, you must have one of the following:

a) One full year of graduate study in a business administration curriculum

b) One year of experience in the review, analysis and evaluation of managerial policies, practices, systems or procedures

c) The Superior Academic Achievement provisions for GS-7 Accountant Auditor with a major in a business administration curriculum including 6 semester hours in accounting and auditing subjects.

GS-9

The experience and training requirements for GS-7 (above) plus one additional year of experience in the review, analysis and evaluation of managerial policies, practices, systems or procedures *or*

Completion of all the requirements for a master's degree with a major in business administration or public administration which included or was supplemented by 6 semester hours in accounting or auditing at the graduate or undergraduate level.

Note: Reprinted from a U.S. General Accounting Office recruiting bulletin (General Accounting Office, October 28, 1973).

The annual salary for entrance-level trainees in 1976 was about $11,046 for a GS-7 and about $12,482 for a GS-9. Over one-third of GAO's professional staff is supervisory and mangement jobs at grades GS-13 through 18. Salaries for these jobs range from $24,308 to $39,600 as of October 1976. Salary adjustments are made from time to time to remain comparable with the private sector.[2] There are fifteen regional offices of the GAO located throughout the United States, as well as offices in Europe and the Far East.

122   Internal Revenue Service

The Internal Revenue Service (IRS) recruits accounting graduates as trainee internal auditors and as internal revenue agents. Agents can expect to move up from the trainee level to the GS-11 grade within three years. Currently, of the fourteen to fifteen thousand agents working at IRS, more than eleven thousand are at grades GS-11, 12, 13, and 14. The salary range of these jobs as of October 1976 was $17,056 to $22,177

---

2. U.S. Civil Service Commission, *Accountants, Auditors and IRS Agents, Announcement No. 425* (rev. January 1977), p. 2.

annually for a GS-11 and $28,725 to $37,347 for a GS-14.[3] Federal salaries have been increased since the publication of this range of salaries.

123 Federal Bureau of Investigation

The Federal Bureau of Investigation (FBI) is one of the many federal, state, and local law enforcement agencies concerned with "white-collar crime." The losses through bank fraud and embezzlement have increased rapidly during the past years. In 1969 the reported losses were $32,869,000; in 1973, $135,609,000.[4] There have also been increased violations of the federal bank robbery statute.

The FBI agent accountants play a key role in the program against white-collar crime. The FBI has initiated a series of seminars to prepare agent accountants to recognize and cope with the new methods used in band fraud and embezzlement of funds. The cost to the nation may be in excess of $40 billion each year, excluding price fixing and industrial sabotage.[5]

Information concerning the position of special agents in the FBI and their training and salary is given in Exhibit 1-5.

Exhibit 1-5
Information Concerning the Position of Special Agent in the Federal Bureau of Investigation

---

The Federal Bureau of Investigation is the primary investigative arm of the United States Department of Justice and, as such, its jurisdiction includes a wide range of responsibilities in the criminal, civil, and security fields. An additional responsibility is the correlation of information concerning the internal security of the United States and dissemination of such data to interested agencies in the Executive Branch of the Federal Government.

Training and Salary
The Special Agent position is not under Civil Service appointment regulations. All appointments in this service are made on a probationary basis and become permanent upon the satisfactory completion of a one-year period. Applicants receiving an appointment must satisfactorily complete a course of training at the FBI Academy located at Quantico, Virginia, which is approximately 15 weeks in duration. Following this training, the appointee is assigned to a field office. The entrance salary for Special Agents is $14,824 per annum and they are paid their regular salary while attending the New Agents' Training School. Following assignment to a field office, additional compensation in the amount of $3,706.00 per year may be earned for overtime performance as required in connection with official duties and provided the performance of the Agent in this regard meets certain necessary official requirements. Since all promotions are based on demonstrated merit rather than seniority, excellent opportunities for advancement exist. While engaged in investigative work, Special Agents can earn as much as $29,782 yearly, exclusive of overtime, and many Agents promoted to supervisory positions receive even higher salaries.

Note: Reprinted from Federal Bureau of Investigation pamphlet FD-257 (rev. October 24, 1975.).

3. Ibid.
4. U.S. Department of Justice, Federal Bureau of Investigation, *Know Your FBI* (rev. October 1974), p. 5.
5. James Nolan, "FBI Agent Accountants Intensify Campaign Against 'White Collar' Crime," *Journal of Accountancy* (October 1974), pp. 26, 28, 30.

124 Department of Defense Audit Agencies

Department of Defense Audit Agencies include the Defense Contract Audit Agency, Auditor General, Defense Supply Agency, U.S. Army Audit Agency, Naval Audit Service, and Auditor General, U.S. Air Force. These agencies are responsible for the review and appraisal of military installations around the world and of private firms and universities that are conducting research, construction, or manufacturing projects under defense contracts.

125 Other Federal Agencies

The Department of Health, Education, and Welfare (HEW) employs accountants to work as auditors to review programs that affect the lives of millions of Americans. HEW also has an audit effort involving the internal management of the department itself as well as agencies having HEW contracts and grants. There are many regulatory agencies, such as the Securities and Exchange Commission and the Federal Power Commission, that require the services of accountants.

Exhibit 1-6 indicates where the accountant may find jobs with the federal government.

Exhibit 1-6
Where Most Accountant Graduates Work

	Number
Department of Agriculture	1,400
Civil Aeronautics Board	60
Department of Commerce	240
Department of Defense—	
Department of the Air Force	1,800
Department of the Army	3,100
Department of the Navy	1,300
Defense Contract Audit Agency	3,000
Defense Supply Agency	450
Federal Power Commission	110
General Accounting Office	2,350
General Services Administration	240
Department of Health, Education and Welfare	1,000
Department of Housing and Urban Development	500
Department of the Interior	400
Interstate Commerce Commission	90
Department of Labor	130
National Aeronautics & Space Administration	300
Office of Economic Opportunity	100
Post Office Department	230
Securities and Exchange Commission	70
Small Business Administration	80
State Department	400
Department of Transportation	560
Department of the Treasury	15,200

Note: Reprinted from *Accountants, Auditors, and IRS Agents,* Announcement No. 425 (U.S. Civil Service Commission, May 1975), p. 3.

130 POSITIONS WITH STATE GOVERNMENT

State and local governments may use the registers established for the recruiting of federal government employees as a means of recruiting qualified candidates for jobs within their own organizations. However, if you are specifically interested in employment with a local government agency, you should apply directly to the proper jurisdiction.

By the mid-1980s, employment in state and local government is expected to reach 19.5 million, an increase of more than 35 percent over the 14.5 million employed in 1974.[6]

The *College Placement Annual, 1976*, in its survey of monthly beginning salary offers, indicated a high of $996, a low of $768, and an average of $852 for accounting positions in local and state governments. Positions are available as accountants, bank examiners, internal auditors, mineral royalty auditors, revenue auditors, revenue agents, tax commission auditors, budget analysts, and in many other classifications. Pay is usually competitive with industry relative to the work requirements.

State and local governments ordinarily have retirement programs, either in conjunction with social security or, in some cases, independent of the federal social security system. Retirement benefits are usually provided from funds contributed by the employee and by the governmental unit.

140 POSITIONS IN TEACHING

Teaching, the largest profession, employed 2.7 million full-time teachers in all fields in 1973-74. In addition to the 2.7 million employed in the elementary and secondary schools and in colleges and universities, thousands taught part-time.[7] The part-time instructors included accountants, scientists, physicians, and many other professionals.

141 High Schools and Vocational Schools

The need for secondary teachers is expected to increase only slightly in the 1980s. Most teaching positions will be generated from the need to replace those who retire or leave the profession. In some areas, however, a continuing teacher shortage is evident. There is a shortage of vocational-technical subject teachers. Accounting teachers are included in this group.

In the school year 1973-74, in public school systems enrolling 6,000 or more pupils, beginning teachers with bachelor's degrees earned an average salary of $7,720; beginning teachers with master's degrees earned an average of $8,586.[8]

---

6. U.S. Dept. of Labor, *Occupational Outlook Handbook*, 1976-77 ed., p. 14.
7. Ibid., p. 206.
8. Ibid., p. 208.

142 Colleges and Universities

About 30 percent of all persons in the United States between 18 and 21 years of age attended college in 1974. In the same year about 620,000 teachers worked in more than 2,600 colleges and universities. About 399,000 — nearly two-thirds — were full-time senior staff. The remainder was made up of part-time senior staff, full-time junior instructors, teaching fellows, teaching assistants, and laboratory assistants.[9]

The demand for college and university teachers is expected to continue to expand. The supply of new master's and doctor's degree graduates is expected to more than meet this increase in most areas. The demand for instructors in accounting is somewhat greater than that of most other disciplines. "There is no 'Ph.D. glut' in the field of accountancy. Rather, it is likely that there will be in the immediate two to three years ahead a growing scarcity of qualified doctoral candidates available for positions."[10] There is a tendency of colleges and universities to restrict new hires, when possible, to Ph.D.'s.[11]

In a report on the supply and demand for accounting faculty made by the American Accounting Association, the following salary range for the 1977-78 academic year for new faculty without previous full-time experience was predicted:[12]

Salary	With Doctorate	Without Doctorate
Under $15,000	10	45
$15,000-15,999	8	18
16,000-16,999	17	27
17,000-17,999	34	34
18,000-18,999	73	43
19,000-19,999	65	18
20,000 or more	27	1
	234	186

150 POSITIONS WITH NATIONAL CPA FIRMS

The practice of a national CPA firm may be carried on throughout the United States by offices located in many major cities. Such a CPA firm may also be a multinational copartnership with offices located throughout the United States and in many foreign countries. The senior partner is responsible for the supervision of all functions of the partnership, subject

---

9. Ibid. p. 210-211.
10. William F. Crum, "Newest Survey of Doctoral Programs in Accounting." *Journal of Accountancy* (October 1974), p. 103.
11. U.S. Department of Labor, *Occupational Outlook*, p. 212.
12. Paul L. Gerhardt, *1976-77 Report on Supply and Demand for Accounting Professors* (Sarasota, Fla.: American Accounting Association, January 1977), p. 6.

to the advice and consent of an executive committee. The individual partners are ultimately responsible for all of the firm's activities, as guided by the senior partner.

151 General Information

A large firm may be organized as shown in Exhibit 1-7. In a multinational firm there will probably be a partner in charge of the foreign operations.

Exhibit 1-7
Organization of a Large CPA Firm

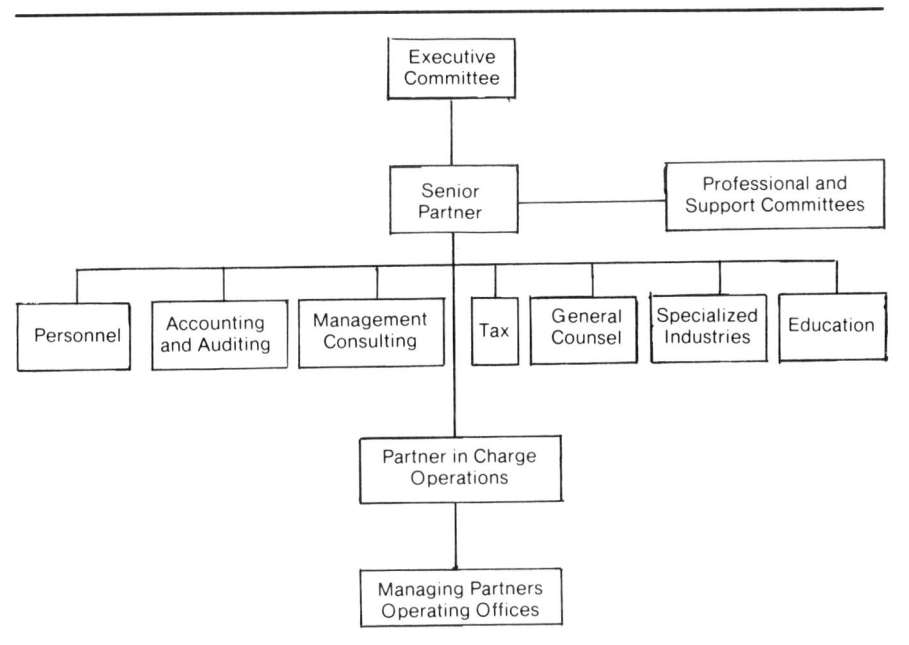

```
                    Executive
                    Committee
                        |
                        |
                    Senior ———————— Professional and
                    Partner          Support Committees
    _____|_____
    |         |          |        |       |         |          |
Personnel  Accounting  Management Tax  General  Specialized  Education
           and Auditing Consulting      Counsel  Industries
                        |
                Partner in Charge
                   Operations
                        |
                Managing Partners
                 Operating Offices
```

A new employee may be given a title of assistant staff accountant or its equivalent, and the path of promotion could be as follows:[13]

Title	Years in Grade	Cumulative Years
Assistant Staff Accountant	1-2	
Staff Accountant	1-2	2-4
Senior Accountant	1-2	3-6
Supervisory Senior Accountant	1-2	4-8
Supervisor	1-2	5-10
Manager	2-3	7-13
Partner/Principal		

---

13. Material presented is from information provided by a national public accounting firm. Used by permission.

Lawyers may become partners in some firms. Professionals other than CPAs and lawyers with CPA firms are given the title *principal* rather than *partner*. But the other steps in promotion are the same. The usual time with a firm before being promoted to partner is about 10 or 11 years.

The range of pay in summary form for CPAs with national firms in May 1976 was approximately as follows:[14]

Staff Accountants	$12,000 to $17,000
Seniors	$15,000 to $21,000
Managers	$23,000 to $45,000
Partners	$65,000 and up

A first year's typical assignment with a national firm may be as shown in Exhibit 1-8.

Exhibit 1-8
Typical First Year Assignments

Staff Training (2 weeks)
Attended Audit Level I training in local office during first week of employment. Completed Audit Level II training with new staff members from other offices at one of [the] regional training centers. Emphasis was on learning by doing rather than lectures.

Medium-Sized Manufacturing Company (3 weeks)
Assisted in the interim examination. Worked closely with the in-charge senior in analyzing income and expense accounts. Also, selected customer accounts for confirmation and controlled client's computer preparation of customer statements

Electronics Manufacturer (2 days)
Participated in physical inventory observation at one of the client's plants. The inventory consisted of more than 100,000 separate items and the selection of test counts was done by statistical sampling techniques.

Ethical Drug Manufacturer (3 weeks)
Assisted management consultants gather data for the design and installation of a computer system. Assignment required a review of billing and purchase procedures and attendance at a seminar given by the EDP equipment manufacturer to ascertain system capabilities.

Staff Training (2 days)
Attended in-house seminar conducted by members of staff and management. Discussed new opinions relating to generally accepted accounting principles. The managing partner of the office discussed the recently concluded annual partners' meeting. The seminar ended with a cocktail party and dinner.

Machine Tool Manufacturer (6 weeks)
Assignment consisted of the review and completion of Internal Control Questionnaire, tailoring of the standard audit program guide to the client's system, and performing interim audit procedures for cash, inventory, and fixed assets. Spent quite some time drafting and polishing comments about these audit procedures for inclusion in letter of management on internal control. This major machine tool manufacturer operates in 15 other countries through the use of foreign subsidiary companies and sales branches.

14. Ibid.

Exhibit 1-8 (continued)

Tax Department (1 week)
Assigned to tax department to assist in developing background information for a tax research problem. Client was considering the initiation of a stock option plan, had requested presentation of the alternatives available.

Illness (4 days)
Unable to work due to illness. Time fully compensated by employer.

Shoe Manufacturer (3 weeks)
Participated in an audit engagement for a new client considering an initial public offering of securities. One of the engagement requirements was an examination of the income statement for the three prior years. This necessitated a thorough review of the client's inventory.

Medium-Sized Manufacturing Company (4 weeks)
Returned to client for completion of the audit. For first time, participated in preparation of financial statements and also assisted in drafting letter to management concerning improvements in internal control. At the client's request, assisted the Treasurer in the preparation of their Federal and State corporate income tax returns.

Electronics Manufacturer (2 weeks)
Again returned to a client and assisted in the completion of the annual audit. On the third day of the audit the client's sprinkler system accidentally became operative. Judging by the condition of the workpapers and my suit the sprinkler system functions very well indeed.

Career Planning Discussion (1 day)
Met with a manager who has been in charge of most of my engagements to discuss my overall progress with the firm and to begin to formulate a plan of assignments and training in line with my expressed career objectives. This was the first of many such meetings that will take place throughout my career.

Management Assistance Program (2 days)
Participated in Management Assistance Program helping a minority group businessman prepare his financial statements for a loan application.

Machine Tool Manufacturer (5 weeks)
Returned for year-end audit. Updated interim working papers, analyzed various balance sheet accounts, and performed audit of small subsidiary that will be included in consolidated financial statements.

Clothing Manufacturer (4 weeks)
Assisted in the advance planning of the audit for this client. Assignment included reviewing and preparing flow charts of the client's operating procedures. The flow charts were designed to provide an overview of the operations and possible weaknesses in internal control.

Commercial Bank (5 days)
Participated in surprise cash and securities counts on three commercial banks. We had been requested by the Examining Committees of the Boards of Directors to assist them in their annual surprise examination.

Software Company (3 weeks)
Involved in the initial audit and SEC registration work of a computer software company planning to go public. The client had incurred significant initial programming costs which they proposed to defer. It was necessary to determine the nature of the costs and the prospect of recoverability of these costs from future operations.

Staff Training (1 week)
Attended a course which provided me with additional computer knowledge and taught me to use the Firm's generalized computer auditing program. This course was held at a Professional Development Center.

Exhibit 1-8 (continued)

University (3 weeks)
Took part in examination of annual financial statements. Since the audit required knowledge of fund accounting, I attended a three-day institutional staff training course conducted by members of the staff management group with expertise in this area.

CPA Exam (3 days)
Sat for CPA examination. Time fully compensated by employer. When I learn that I passed the examination, fees will be reimbursed by my employer and I may receive some monetary recognition of this accomplishment.

Vacation (2 weeks)

Electric Wire and Cable Manufacturer (5 weeks)
Assisted in special acquisition audit of a company being acquired by a client. Assignments included reviewing fixed assets, manufacturing costs, and comparative income analysis. The financial statements will be one consideration affecting the determination of the ultimate purchase price.

Chemical Manufacturer (1 week)
Participated in completion of forms which were sent to data center for processing and matching of inventory test counts to client's inventory computer records. Reviewed report prepared by data center and cleared all exceptions.

Career Planning Discussion (1 day)
Met again with manager for my second semi-annual discussion. We reviewed my first year progress and performance and discussed my career plans for the future.

Note: Reprinted by permission from a brochure developed by a national public accounting firm.

Business Week made an estimate of the Big Eight operations. This estimate is shown in Exhibit 1-9. The term *Big Eight* refers to the eight largest CPA firms in the United States.

**Exhibit 1-9
Accounting's Big Eight Firms: A Capsule View**

Firm and Home Office	Major Clients		Estimated U.S. Net Billings
Arthur Andersen & Co. Chicago	ITT, Texaco, General Telephone, Kraftco, Tenneco, Occidental Petroleum, General Dynamics, Marcor, United Airlines, Commonwealth Edison. Audits 380 companies on New York and American stock exchanges.	41 U.S. offices 650 U.S. partners and principals	$190-million 65% audit 17.5% tax 17.5% consulting
Ernst & Ernst Cleveland	Ling-Temco-Vought, McDonnell Douglas, R. J. Reynolds, Gulf & Western, Coca-Cola, TRW, BankAmerica, Western Bancorporation, Ashland Oil, Republic Steel. Audits 265 companies on New York and American stock exchanges.	108 U.S. offices 390 U.S. partners and principals	$180-million 60% audit 20% tax 20% consulting
Haskins & Sells New York	General Motors, Procter & Gamble, International Harvester, North American Rockwell, Continental Can, Monsanto, A&P, Southern Pacific, TWA, Pacific Gas & Electric. Audits 245 companies on New York and American stock exchanges.	75 U.S. offices 400 U.S. partners and principals	$155-million 70% audit 20% tax 10% consulting
Lybrand, Ross Bros. & Montgomery New York	AT&T, Ford, Atlantic Richfield, Firestone, Sun Oil, American Can, Sperry Rand, Alcoa, Kroger, Pan American. Audits 260 companies on New York and American stock exchanges.	70 U.S. offices 450 U.S. partners and principals	$135-million 78% audit 17% tax 5% consulting
Peat, Marwick, Mitchell & Co. New York	General Electric, Singer, Burlington Industries, Xerox, Cities Service, Beatrice Foods, First National City, Chase Manhattan, Safeway, Penney. Audits 330 companies on New York and American stock exchanges.	106 U.S. offices 660 U.S. partners and principals	$225-million 65% audit 20% tax 15% consulting
Price Waterhouse & Co. New York	Standard Oil [N.J.], IBM, Gulf Oil, U.S. Steel, Westinghouse, Standard Oil of Calif., Standard Oil [Ind.], Dupont, Shell, Consolidated Edison. Audits 350 companies on New York and American stock exchanges.	54 U.S. offices 250 U.S. partners and principals	$180-million 70% audit 18% tax 12% consulting
Touche Ross & Co. New York	Chrysler, Boeing, Greyhound, Litton, Sears, Mead, Federated Department Stores, Jewel Cos., Prudential, American Motors. Audits 150 companies on New York and American stock exchanges.	60 U.S. offices 450 U.S. partners and principals	$110-million 58% audit 25% tax 17% consulting
Arthur Young & Co. New York	Mobil Oil, Western Electric, RCA, Swift, Continental Oil, Lockheed, Phillips Petroleum, Textron, American-Standard, American Airlines. Audits 160 companies on New York and American stock exchanges.	60 U.S. offices 370 U.S. partners and principals	$100-million 66% audit 17% tax 17% consulting

Note: Reprinted from the April 22, 1972 issue of *Business Week* by special permission. 1972 by McGraw-Hill, Inc.

152 Accounting And Auditing

The rules of the American Institute of Certified Public Accountants (AICPA), state societies of CPAs, and the Securities and Exchange Commission (SEC) regulate the professional conduct of accounting and auditing practitioners. A cooperative effort by all members of the professional staff is required to ensure that the rules of the regulatory bodies are followed and that a responsible audit and report is made.

The team approach is used in audit engagements in order that a number of highly trained and qualified professionals are able to cover all key areas with thoroughness and that the standards for auditing and reporting are met.

The responsibilities of the members of the audit teams are described in Exhibit 1-10.

Exhibit 1-10

THE AUDIT TEAM
The team approach to the audit engagement is designed to bring to each engagement the resources of a number of highly qualified professionals, who will cover all areas of the audit with thoroughness while ensuring that each step in the audit process is subjected to the judgment and review of several members of the team. Normally the audit team (often assisted by tax and management consulting personnel) consists of the audit staff, in-charge accountant, manager/supervisor, and audit engagement partner, as well as the preissuance reviewing partner and other partners within the Firm who may be consulted in regard to particular accounting, auditing or specialized industry matters. While each member of the audit team has somewhat different responsibilities, one responsibility that is common to all members is that of keeping other members of the team informed about the progress of the engagement. This is necessary to help ensure that all matters of significance receive professional consideration by the proper member of the team.

Briefly, the responsibilities of each member of the audit team are as follows:

Audit Engagement Partner
The audit engagement partner has the ultimate responsibility for the audit engagement. He determines the content of the Accountants' Report issued on completion of the engagement and commits the Firm to the report by signing the Firm's name. Therefore, he is responsible for ascertaining that Firm and professional standards have been complied with throughout the engagement. Specifically, the audit engagement partner is responsible for the planning of the engagement, resolution of any technical accounting or auditing problems that arise in the course of the engagement, evaluation of the audit work performed, review of the financial statements related to the engagement, and, finally, signing of the Accountants' Report.

Audit Manager/Supervisor
The audit manager/supervisor is responsible for supervising the personnel performing the audit. He plans the audit engagement in cooperation with the audit engagement partner and the in-charge accountant, ensures that all individuals involved in the audit are cognizant of the audit plan, and supervises the successful performance of the plan. He reviews all working papers prepared for the engagement. Inherent in his review procedures is the fact that he evaluates the reasonableness of all conclusions reached by the audit personnel preparing the working papers.

Exhibit 1-10 (continued)

In-Charge Accountant
The in-charge accountant is involved in the overall planning of the engagement and directs the day-to-day functioning of the audit plan. He is responsible for instructing and supervising the audit staff assigned to the engagement and for reviewing in detail all the working papers prepared by the audit staff for adequacy of documentation and for the reasonableness of the conclusions they have reached.

In-charge accountants also have the responsibility to discuss all accounting and auditing problems with the engagement manager/supervisor and to obtain the manager's/supervisor's concurrence with their conclusions. At the completion of the engagement, the in-charge accountant states in writing his conclusion as to the adequacy of the audit working papers (including programs and questionnaires) in support of the financial statements and reports issued and as to their compliance with Firm and professional standards.

Audit Staff
Each audit staff member is responsible for performing the procedures outlined in the audit program for the engagement. He is responsible for the adequacy and propriety of the working papers he produces and the conclusions he reaches. The staff member is responsible for informing the in-charge accountant of all accounting and auditing problems he encounters.

THE AUDIT EXAMINATION
The following represent the major steps in the logic process which an auditor uses in approaching an audit engagement:
1. Obtain an overall understanding of the client's business, including the economy, industry, client's position in the industry, and detailed knowledge of the client's operations and background.
2. Based on that understanding, make analytical reviews of financial and operating data and identify major areas of audit concern (e.g., inventory obsolescence, receivable collectibility, revenue recognition, etc.).
3. Determine the major audit objectives in the identified areas of audit concern.
4. Obtain an in-depth understanding of the client's accounting and internal control system, particularly in those areas related to the identified audit concerns.
5. Identify the internal control strengths and weaknesses which have a bearing on the audit objectives.
6. Finally, develop a tailored audit program which is responsive to the audit concerns and which gives recognition to the evaluation of the internal control system.

Note: Reprinted by permission from a brochure developed by a national public accounting firm.

153 Taxes

Tax laws are under continual change. Tax reform acts that are approved may clear one problem area, but often open other questions with increasing complexity. In addition, taxes are used as an instrument of economic policy or social policy, as in the case of investment credit. The investment credit provision has been enacted, suspended, reinstated, repealed and reenacted in accordance with the lawmaker's view of the state of the economy.

The following paragraphs describe the tax services offered by a national CPA firm.

[The Human Interest]

Most of our tax practice is involved with people. Whether serving an individual or a company, we are constantly working with human nature and human problems, and the situations are of endless variety. As examples:

...a client may wish to sell his business rather than leave it to a son whose judgement he doesn't trust. What is the best procedure?

...another client may want to enable certain long-time employees (but not all employees) to acquire stock in his company. Is this feasible?

...wealthy clients may want to make large contributions to charity, without penalizing their heirs. What are the tax consequences?

...others, who have heard of tax benefits possible by investing in wildcat oil ventures, ask us for advice.

...clients seeking divorces often bring complicated tax problems to us for resolution.

In such situations, as the tax consultant, you're the "doctor."

In brief, while we are guided by the statutes, we work with people and their daily problems. The hopes, as well as the concerns, of our clients are entwined in our work. And the resulting problems are resolved by reconciling their human needs and objectives with the technical tax issues involved.

[The Future Outlooks]

Today a CPA's tax responsibilities involve daily consideration of taxes as they affect business decisions. Virtually every transaction has a possible tax effect, favorable or unfavorable.

Corporate acquisitions, compensation plans, family tax planning—anything which concerns money involves tax considerations, usually with a choice of alternatives.

We must evaluate the pluses and minuses of each alternative and define the possibilities. Sometimes, we urge a specific course. Always, we make sure that the client understands the available options and the probable consequences of each.

For a client who plans to acquire another company, we will define the relative advantages of a stock versus asset acquisition, based upon the allocation of the purchase price, any net operating loss or other carry-overs present, investment credit or depreciation recaptures, and other factors.

Similarly, we make studies for clients on tax incentives available in proposed investments, the tax aspects of operating abroad, changes in accounting methods, and consolidated returns. All of these are major problem areas on which the Treasury Department has concentrated during recent years. We practice tax accounting, not tax law. We adhere fully to the joint statement regarding tax practice adopted by the American Institute of CPA's in cooperation with the American Bar Association.

As CPA's, we represent clients at all administrative levels of Federal and state tax authorities. We gather data for revenue agent examinations through research, client discussion, review of audit papers, and conferences with the client's legal counsel as advisable—and where necessary, we prepare written protests against the findings of the examining agent. We secure advance rulings from the Internal Revenue Service on various proposed transactions. By policy, however, we do not practice before the Tax Court.

[Preparation]

Some of our tax people transfer from our audit staff. Others enter our Division directly upon graduation.

Primarily, they are business school or law school graduates. Naturally, all must have real interest in tax work. We expect law graduates to have a thorough knowledge of accounting.

In auditing, our people are constantly involved in tax matters, so that they find some working knowledge of taxes a necessity. If they become deeply interested and show some flair for tax practice, they usually can transfer to our Tax Division.

Legal training develops a keen analytical sense which is most useful in solving tax problems.

A combination of accounting knowledge and legal training is excellent for tax work.

Various other educational backgrounds are also suitable. A great deal depends on the depth of interest.

[Training for Tax Service Area]

- Firm-wide Audit Staff Training School—for new staff, a 3-week course, usually attended during the first month or two with the firm.
- Basic U.S. Tax School—during your first year, a 2-week course stressing concepts of Federal income, gift, and estate taxation.
- Intermediate U.S. Tax Sxhool—during your second year, a 2-week course emphasizing corporation income taxes.

Additionally, we regularly conduct a number of Specialized Tax Courses relating to particular areas—such as tax problems peculiar to certain industries, and special tax areas such as reorganizations, international taxation, and family tax planning. You will have opportunities to attend. In addition, each local office holds regular training sessions.

All training is under the personal supervision of tax partners and managers, and is related to their practical experience.

As you progress, you will have opportunity to participate in tax forums. You will be encouraged to write for tax publications and address groups on tax subjects.

In addition to our extensive library resources, our offices throughout the world share their experience in tax work through our Tax Subject File. This File, available in every office, contains thousands of examples of significant tax experiences encountered by us in our tax practice. It is an invaluable resource.

Your next training step is always available, dependent only on your readiness.[15]

---

15. Used by permission and adapted.

154 Management Advisory Services

Management advisory service, sometimes called administrative service, is provided to thousands of clients each year by public accounting firms. The professional services are provided by conducting studies and by designing and installing systems and procedures to produce information needed by management in directing a broad range of activities.

The following examples illustrate the engagements that have been handled by the management advisory services staff of a large national CPA firm:

- For a large manufacturer—Developed a financial model to evaluate alternative acquistion strategies.
- For an insurance company—Developed a system whereby executive management could control the activities of systems development personnel.
- For a worldwide conglomerate — Developed a uniform system of reporting financial and operating results for the many subsidiaries.
- For a carpet manufacturer — Assisted in evaluation of potential alternative manufacturing facilities.
- For a school system—Designed and installed a comprehensive real-time system for scheduling and assignment of teaching personnel.
- For a hospital—Designed and installed a planning model to assist in their expansion program.
- For a retail chain—Designed and installed a real-time computer system for stock replenishment.
- For a city planning commission—Designed and implemented a data base which describes the city and its residents to be used to plan urban projects.
- For a stock exchange—Assisted in installation of a computerized system to make settlements among brokers.
- For a university—Assisted in developing a long-range systems plan for course/curriculum, student and financial information.
- For an electronics manufacturer—Designed and installed computerized data collection from the manufacturing floor.[16]

160 POSITIONS WITH LOCAL CPA FIRMS

A position with a large local firm may be very similar to that with a national firm. The new recruit will usually serve as an assistant on fairly large engagements. As experience and competence are gained, the individual will move up the ladder to an in-charge role on small engagements, then on larger engagements. This approach enables the professional to gain a better grasp of the total picture than would a long period in the role of an assistant.

---

16. From a brochure developed by a national public accounting firm. Used by permission.

161 Auditing

A new employee with a good college record may expect to advance to light senior in about two years and to heavy senior in four years. From that point, becoming a partner varies with individual capacity, interest, ability, and the needs of the firm. Usually there is no arbitrary limit as to the age of recruits, times for advancement, or number of partners to be admitted into a firm.

The clients of a large local firm ordinarily include a cross section of the business community. They include building contractors, subcontractors, manufacturers, retailers, wholesalers, municipalities, and financial institutions. The clients may require opinion audits; however, there will be needs for tax and management advisory services as well.

162 Tax

The related tax work may be considered a part of an audit engagement, and the accountant-client discussions that result may bring forth additional services of a mangement advisory nature. Each professional on the staff of a local CPA firm may be required to establish some degree of proficiency in tax return preparation. There may also be a tax group to provide in-depth support.

163 Management Advisory Service

Management advisory services may be assigned to the in-charge auditor. There may or may not be other professionals available to add support to the audit team in management advisory service. Again, in the local firm the professional will very likely be required to develop some degree of proficiency in this area.

164 Write-Up

Many local firms provide a write-up (bookkeeping) service for their clients. The client in a manner prescribed by the CPA firm accumulates the business transactions. From time to time the documents representing the transactions are collected and posted (or keypunched if a computer is used), and financial statements are prepared for the client. The financial statements may be delivered to the client for review and analysis or the CPA firm may also be involved in their analysis. Write-up work and the financial statements from that write-up work may be a significant part of a local firm's business.

165 Professional Development

During the first two years of employment the recruit will most likely be exposed to a wide variety of opportunities to learn from on-the-job training. The in-charge accountant will be expected to guide the beginner, carefully review his or her work, and offer suggestions and directions. The new employee may be required to attend the ten-day course developed by the AICPA after about six months of experience.

The new employee will be expected to prepare for and take the CPA examination. This is usually a rsponsibility of the individual. Some guidance in methods of preparation is usually made available by the firm.

170 POSITIONS IN INDUSTRY

Greater use of accounting information in business management, changing tax systems, and growth of large corporations that must provide financial reports to stockholders all point to excellent opportunities for accountants. The expanding use of data processing systems may reduce the demand for lower level or paraprofessional accountants. However, this same trend may place an increasing demand on the supply of highly trained accountants to administer and analyze the information generated by such systems.[17]

The monthly beginning salaries offered in the Accounting/Auditing functional area as reported by the College Placement Survey report of July 1977 are presented in Exhibit 1-11.

Exhibit 1-11
Beginning Salaries in the Accounting/Auditing Functional Area

Employer	No. Offers Reported	80 Per Cent High	80 Per Cent Low	Avg. $
Business	4,736	$1,217	$933	$1,075
Manufacturing/Industrial	1,327	1,199	987	1,048
Government—Federal	69	1,072	726	899
Government—Local/State	123	1,140	796	968
Non-Profit Organizations	42	1,015	705	860
All Employers	6,297	$1,214	$914	$1,064
BACHELOR'S LEVEL All Employers	6,320	$1,217	$907	$1,062
MASTER'S LEVEL All Employers	751	$1,408	$1,086	$1,247

Note: Reprinted by permission of the publisher from *CPC Salary Survey* (Bethlehem, Pa.: College Placement Council, July 1977).

"CPC Salary Survey: A Study of Beginning Offers." The beginning salary data reported are based on offers (not acceptances) to graduating students in selected curricula and graduate programs during the normal college recruiting period, September to June. The Survey covers job openings in a broad range of functional areas, *except teaching,* within employing organizations in business, industry, and government. The data are submitted by a representative group of colleges throughout the United States.

17. U.S. Department of Labor, *Occupational Outlook,* p. 125.

The individual holding a degree in accounting can expect to be a viable candidate for a position in almost any area of business. The person trained in costing concepts is well prepared to assist the marketing manager, for example, in the pricing of products, product selection, and in product mix determinations. Completion of the courses in the accounting curriculum will provide the graduate with the basic knowledge to secure positions in the following areas:

Budget Analysis
Budget Control
Budget Planning
Controllership
Cost Accounting
Cost-Benefit Analysis
Credit Management
Earnings Forecasting
Economic Analysis
Equipment Accounting
Financial Planning
Hotel and Restaurant Accounting
Internal Auditing
Inventory Analysis
Inventory Control
Management Advisory Service

Merchandise Control
Merchandise Procurement
Oil and Gas Accounting
Operation Research
Organization Planning
Pension Fund Administration
Plant Accounting
Product Costing and Pricing
Purchasing
Systems Design
Systems Survey and Analysis
Systems Installation
Tax Planning
Wage and Benefit Analysis
Warehouse Operation

Industry, regardless of its product or service, has a need for persons trained in accounting. Those needs will be found in almost all of the organizational and functional areas within the individual company.

Typical entry level position descriptions in industry for both bachelor's and master's degree holders in accounting include the following:

Accounting and Information Services

Education requirements: Bachelors degree with emphasis in finance or accounting.

For those who enter the accounting function directly, training is on the job. Initial positions cover general, revenue or financial accounting. Assignments include preparation of accounting entries, development of reports and control of data flow to and from the computer.

Systems Analysis

Educational requirements: Bachelors or Masters degree in computer science, business or mathematics.

Activities in systems analysis include feasibility studies and evaluation analyses, and design and implementation of new or improved systems. Vital to this function is the ability to understand the needs of the organization and to translate these requirements into appropriate and useful system concepts.

Controllership and Financial Management

Educational requirements: MBA (or occasionally Bachelors) degree with emphasis in finance or accounting.

Training for controllership and financial management is largely informal and on the job. At the corporate level, these functions provide advice and guidance to management and administer policies and controls relating to the management of the Company's financial affairs. Activities include profit planning, budgeting, performance analysis, capital administration, corporate investments and tax.

Accounting and Administrative Development Programs

Educational requirements: Bachelors degree with emphasis in finance or accounting.

The development programs for accounting and administrative activities involve eighteen to twenty-four months of rotational assignments designed to expose new employees to various functions and departments. Depending on the unit entered, the program may include investments, joint operations accounting, revenue accounting, wholesale processing, data processing, general accounting, financial accounting, and planning and evaluation.

Auditing

Educational requirements: Bachelors degree in business-related disciplines.

Auditors work at various office and field locations conducting complete financial and operational audits of company-wide activities. Considerable travel is often required. The primary function of the auditing group is to help management appraise its goals, policies, and procedures, and to suggest improvements where necessary. Speaking and writing well are a must.

Programming

Educational requirements: Bachelors or Masters degree in computer science, business or mathematics.

Programmers develop detailed logic to effectively convert a set of general program specifications into a workable problem solution. Developed logic is then translated to computer language.[18]

The candidate who is successful in meeting the challenges of the entry level positions and shows and aptitude for greater responsibility may be promoted to one of the following typical positions.

Departmental Management

Within each accounting-related department there are several levels of management. Moving through these levels is one typical career path for people who begin in accounting, financial analysis or auditing.

Auditing Management

Higher level responsibilities for managing the Company's audit staff and its auditing policies and procedures.

Senior Auditing Positions

More experienced auditors are generally given responsibility tor larger and more important audit assignments and also supervision of audit staffs as needed.

---

18. From "Plan Your Career with Atlantic Richfield," Atlantic Richfield Company. Used by permission.

Departmental Opportunities

Each department and field within the accounting function requires professional staff members. After completing initial assignments, accountants and financial analysts may be assigned to one of these areas.

Senior Analyst Positions

Within the finance-related departments there are several levels of responsibility. More experienced analysts generally have more complex assignments of greater dollar significance.

Senior Systems Analysis Positions

Systems analysts are given additional responsibility through larger, more complex assignments. Advancement also normally means more and more contact with the user in the field.[19]

The next level of positions would probably be reserved for those with exceptional capabilities and vigor. Those positions include the following:

Professional Accounting

For those who want to continue to perform accounting, there are opportunities to remain in the accounting organization, progressing to more senior levels as a specialist.

Other Divisional and Corporate Opportunities

Depending on background, interests and ability there may be opportunities to move to corporate or divisional staffs in fields such as planning, evaluation and other finance-related administrative staffs. Movement to these fields can come from virtually any of the levels and areas described on the chart.

Senior Accounting and Financial Management Opportunities

Higher level managerial responsibilities for the accounting and financial aspects of our business on the divisional or corporate levels.

Management of Systems Analysis or Programming

Higher level responsibility for managing the Company's information systems.

Management of Analytical Functions

Responsibility for the management of financial analysis departments or activities.

Operations Opportunities

People in the systems field may have the opportunity to move into the manufacturing or production fields, particularly if their assignments in systems have been operations-oriented.[20]

19. Ibid.
20. Ibid.

180 MINORITY GROUPS AND WOMEN IN ACCOUNTING

There is a continuing interest by the accounting profession in supporting minority recruitment in government, industry, and in educational programs. These programs are designed to benefit minority ethnic groups as well as women. The U.S. Department of Health, Education and Welfare (HEW) budgeted $150,000 in Title III Funds to support minority recruitment and the equal opportunity committee in its doctoral fellow/visiting scholar program for the academic year 1975-76.[21]

181 Black Accountants

The number of black accountants has been increasing steadily, especially during the past seven years. There were 450 black CPAs in the United States in 1975 compared with 150 in 1968. During this same period, black accountants on the staffs of the largest CPA firms have increased from about one hundred to more than one thousand. The AICPA, various state societies, and the major CPA firms have provided the leadership and opportunity for most of the growth that has occurred. The AICPA Committee on Recruitment and Equal Opportunity has raised over $1.2 million to provide financial assistance to minority group students studying accounting throughout the United States.[22]

The median income of the 206 respondents to a recent survey of black accountants was $24,000; the median for men was $25,000 and for women, $18,000.[23] In addition, black accountants can find a wide market for their talents. The same survey indicated that blacks find employment in industry and government as well as with CPA firms. Exhibit 1-12 indicates the results of the survey.

Exhibit 1-12
Fields of Employment for Blacks

	1975 Survey Male	1975 Survey Female	1975 Survey Total	1968 Survey Total
Public Accounting	111	13	124	29
Teaching	21	6	27	16
Government Accounting	20	2	22	14
Commercial Enterprises	19	2	21	15
Nonprofit Organizations	9	-	9	4
Others	2	2	4	6
Total	182	25	207	84

Source: Bert N. Mitchell, "The Status of the Black CPA—An Update," *Journal of Accountancy* (May 1976), p. 56. Copyright © 1976 by the American Institute of Certified Public Accountants, Inc.

21. AICPA, *Annual Report,* 1974-75.
22. Bert N. Mitchell, "The Status of the Black CPA—An Update," *Journal of Accountancy* (May 1976), pp. 52-54.
23. Ibid., p. 56

182 Women Accountants

In the past few years more and more women have been entering colleges of business, and accounting has received a higher proportion of those women than has any other area. Exhibit 1-13 shows the increasing percentages of business degrees, accounting and nonaccounting, conferred upon women during recent years.

Exhibit 1-13
Percentage of Women Degree Recipients

Year	All Business	Nonaccounting Business Degrees	Accounting Degrees
1966	8.54	9.36	5.94
1968	9.04	9.59	7.15
1970	8.96	8.98	8.87
1972	9.50	9.36	10.01
1973	10.54	10.24	11.70

Source: U.S. Department of Health, Education and Welfare, from Loudell O. Ellis, "Education," *The Woman CPA* (January 1976), p. 14.

From 1967 through 1973 the number of accounting degrees conferred on both men and women in the United States did not increase as rapidly as did those conferred in other areas of business. However, the increasing number of accounting degrees conferred on women more than doubled that of the other business areas. This trend is shown in Exhibit 1-14.

Exhibit 1-14
Annual Increase in the Percentage of Undergraduates Receiving Degrees

Year	All Degrees	Business Degrees Total	Accounting	Women in Accounting
1967	7.06	9.74	3.91	14.47
1968	12.89	15.43	15.18	25.68
1969	14.60	17.62	11.66	25.54
1970	8.25	12.32	5.80	16.83
1971	5.32	8.70	3.48	8.86
1972	1.07	5.01	12.23	20.89
1973	2.02	3.85	12.84	31.35
Total Increase 1966-1973	63.83	95.26	85.37	215.52

Source: U.S. Department of Health, Education and Welfare, from Loudell O. Ellis, "Education," *The Woman CPA* (January 1976), p. 14.

A recent survey was made of junior level undergraduates at the University of Rhode Island concerning factors that may have influenced their decision to major in accounting. A summary of the survey appears in Exhibit 1-15.

Exhibit 1-15
Mean Average Ranking of Factors Influencing Choice of Accounting as Major

Men	Women
1. Salary potential	1. Availability of jobs
2. Courses interesting and challenging	2. Courses interesting and challenging
3. Availability of jobs	3. Quantitative orientation aptitude with numbers
4. Desire for a specialized business background	4. Salary potential
5. Quantitative orientation aptitude with numbers	5. Desire for a specialized business background
6. Influence of family member or friend	6. Influence of family member or friend
7. Prestige of professional status	7. Encouragement of teacher or guidance counselor
8. Encouragement of teacher or guidance counselor	8. Prestige of professional status

Source: Marilyn Weston and Joseph P. Matoney, Jr., "More College Women Majoring in Accounting: The Numbers and Some Reasons," *The Woman CPA* (January 1976), p. 15.

190 CPA ATTORNEYS

Some people have qualified themselves as both an attorney and as a CPA. This is a fairly compatible combination. In many instances it is hard to distinguish where the accounting functions stop and the legal implications begin.

The practice of both public accounting and law was once considered to be unethical by the American Bar Association.[24] This position was later reversed by certain Supreme Court cases.[25] It is now permissible for a dually qualified person to practice both public accounting and law at the same time. The person may not, however, hold himself out to the public in the *joint* capacity of lawyer/CPA. To do so would be a violation of the American Bar Association's *Code of Professional Responsibility and Canons of Judicial Ethics.*

Observations are made by John L. Carey and William O. Doherty concerning the joint practice of accounting and law and of the employment of lawyers by certified public accountants in an AICPA publication, *Ethical Standards of the Accounting Profession.*[26]

---

24. American Bar Association Committee on the Unauthorized Practice of the Law, "Opinion No. 272," *Journal of Accountancy* (October 1946), p. 175
25. Estes v. Telos, 381 U.S. 532, 535 (1965). Williamson v. Lee Optical, Inc., 348 U.S. 483, 489 (1955). Railroad Trainmen v. Virginia Bar, 377 U.S. 6 (1964).
26. John L. Carey and William O. Doherty, *Ethical Standards of the Accounting Profession* (New York: American Institute of Certified Public Accountants, 1966).

2
Professional Examinations

Examinations are needed in all professions to determine if individuals meet the *minimum* standards of the profession. When a CPA audits a client's financial statements and expresses his opinion on the fairness of presentation of those statements, his obligations extend beyond his contract with the client to outside third parties, namely, investors and potential investors. No other profession has this grave obligation to nonclients. Many court cases have emphasized this unique relationship.

210   INFORMATION FOR CPA CANDIDATES

The CPA exam must be taken by all who want to practice public accountancy. One must pass the exam and meet the experience requirements (which vary from state to state) in order to become a certified public accountant. Even those who do not intend to enter the field of public accounting (that is, those that intend to work in industry or government or teaching) in many cases take the exam. There are a number of reasons for this. First, becoming a certified public accountant is considered to be the the mark of a professional. Second, the pay is higher for CPAs than for non-CPAs. Third, being a CPA gives one a wider variety of job opportunities and possibly greater independence.

The CPA exam is prepared by and graded by the American Institute of Certified Public Accountants. A passing grade on any part of the exam is a 75. A typical schedule of the examination involves three days of hard work. The first day is Wednesday and the last day is Friday as follows:

Wednesday	1:30- 6:00 p.m.	Accounting Practice—Part I
Thursday	8:00-12:00 noon	Auditing
Thursday	1:30- 6:00 p.m.	Accounting Practice—Part II
Friday	8:30-12:00 noon	Business Law
Friday	1:30- 5:00 p.m.	Accounting Theory

The exam is administered in most major cities in the United States.

211 State Boards of Accountancy

There are fifty-four areas of jurisdiction in the United States and its possessions that issue regulations concerning the licensing of persons to practice public accounting. These jurisdictions are the fifty states plus the District of Columbia, Guam, Puerto Rico, and the Virgin Islands. Each of these governmental units has established a governing board, usually composed of persons who hold the CPA certificate.

The requirements for taking the CPA examination and receiving the CPA certificate are changed from time to time. Most states require that a candidate hold a bachelor's degree and have certain course requirements in accounting and other business subjects. For the latest requirements for receiving the CPA certificate, write the National Association of State Boards of Accounting (NASBA), 666 Fifth Avenue, New York, New York 10019.

212 Sample CPA Examination Questions and Unofficial Solutions

Selected sample questions from the November 1976 CPA exam are given in Exhibit 2-1. Unofficial solutions are also included.

Exhibit 2-1
Sample CPA Exam Questions

Uniform Certified Public Accountant Examination

(Prepared by the Board of Examiners of the American Institute of Certified Public Accountants and adopted by the examining boards of all states, territories, and the District of Columbia.)

EXAMINATION IN ACCOUNTING PRACTICE — — PART I

November 3, 1976; 1:30 to 6:00 P.M.

NOTE TO CANDIDATES: Suggested time allotments are as follows:

	Estimated Minutes	
All questions are required:	Minimum	Maximum
No. 1	40	50
No. 2	40	50
No. 3	40	50
No. 4	50	60
No. 5	50	60
Total	220	270

Exhibit 2-1 (continued)

INSTRUCTIONS TO CANDIDATES

(Disregard of these instructions may be considered as indicating inefficiency in accounting work.)

1. You must arrange the papers in numerical order of the questions. If more than one page is required for an answer, write "continued" at the bottom of the page. Number pages consecutively. For instance, if 12 pages are used for your answers they should be numbered 1 through 12. The printed answer sheet provided for the objective-type items should be considered to be Page 1.

2. **Enclose all scratch sheets.** Failure to enclose scratch sheets may result in loss of grading points. Scratch sheets need not have page numbers, but you should show the question number and place them immediately following the question to which they relate.

3. Fourteen-column sheets should not be folded until all sheets, both wide and narrow, are place in the proper sequence and fastened together at the top left corner. All fourteen-column sheets should then be wrapped around the back of the papers.

4. A CPA is continually confronted with the necessity of expressing his opinions and conclusions in written reports in clear, unequivocal language. Although the primary purpose of the examination is to test the candidate's knowledge and application of the subject matter, the ability to organize and present such knowledge in acceptable written language will be considered by the examiners.

Note: Material from the Uniform CPA examinations and Unofficial Answers copyright ⓒ 1976 by the American Institute of Certified Public Accountants, Inc., is reprinted with permission.

Number 1 (Estimated time——40 to 50 minutes)

Instructions

Select the **best** answer for each of the following items relating to **a variety of financial-accounting problems.** Use a soft pencil, preferably No. 2, to blacken the appropriate space on the separate printed answer sheet to indicate your answer. **Mark only one answer for each item. Answer all items.** Your grade will be based on your total correct answers.

The following is an example of the manner in which the answer sheet should be marked:

Item

97. Gross billings for merchandise sold by Baker Company to its customers last year amounted to $5,260,000; sales returns and allowances reduced the amounts owed by $160,000. How much were net sales last year for Baker Company?
    a. $4,800,000.
    b. $5,100,000.
    c. $5,200,000.
    d. $5,260,000.

Answer Sheet

97. a. :::::::::: b. ▬▬▬▬ c. :::::::::: d. ::::::::::

Exhibit 2-1 (continued)

Items to be Answered

1. The Dease Company owns a foreign subsidiary with 3,600,000 local currency units (LCU) of property, plant, and equipment before accumulated depreciation at December 31, 1975. Of this amount, 2,400,000 LCU were acquired in 1973 when the rate of exchange was 1.6 LCU to $1, and 1,200,000 LCU were acquired in 1974 when the rate of exchange was 1.8 LCU to $1. The rate of exchange in effect at December 31, 1975, was 2 LCU to $1. The weighted average of exchange rates which were in effect during 1975 was 1.92 LCU to $1. Assuming that the property, plant, and equipment are depreciated using the straight-line method over a ten-year period with no salvage value, how much depreciation expense relating to the foreign subsidiary's property, plant, and equipment should be charged in Dease's income statement for 1975?
   a. $180,000.
   b. $187,500.
   c. $200,000.
   d. $216,667.

2. The Clark Company owns a foreign subsidiary which had net income for the year ended December 31, 1975, of 4,800,000 local currency units (LCU) which was appropriately translated into $800,000. On October 15, 1975, when the rate of exchange was 5.7 LCU to $1, the foreign subsidiary paid a dividend to Clark of 2,400,000 LCU. The dividend represented the net income of the foreign subsidiary for the six months ended June 30, 1975, during which time the weighted average of exchange rates was 5.8 LCU to $1. The rate of exchange in effect at December 31, 1975, was 5.9 LCU to $1. What rate of exchange should be used to translate the dividend for the December 31, 1975, financial statements?
   a. 5.7 LCU to $1.
   b. 5.8 LCU to $1.
   c. 5.9 LCU to $1.
   d. 6.0 LCU to $1.

Items 3 and 4 are based on the following information:

The Marne Company purchased a machine on January 1, 1975, for $900,000 for the express purpose of leasing it. The machine is expected to have a five-year life, no salvage value, and be depreciated on a straight-line basis. On March 1, 1975, Marne leased the machine to the Dal Company for $300,000 a year for a four-year period ending February 28, 1979. Marne incurred total maintenance and other related costs under the provisions of the lease of $15,000 relating to the year ended December 31, 1975. Dal paid $300,000 to Marne on March 1, 1975.

3. Under the operating method, what should be the income before income taxes derived by Marne from this lease for the year ended December 31, 1975?
   a. $55,000.
   b. $70,000.
   c. $85,000.
   d. $100,000.

4. What should be the amount of rent expense incurred by Dal from this lease for the year ended December 31, 1975?
   a. $70,000.
   b. $120,000.
   c. $250,000.
   d. $300,000.

Exhibit 2-1 (continued)

5. The Pasther Company has a contributory pension plan for all of its employees. In 1975, a total of $100,000 was withheld from employee's salaries and deposited into a pension fund administered by an outside trustee. In addition, Pasther deposited $200,000 of its own money into the fund in 1975. Based on the report of Pasther's outside actuaries which was received in December 1975, the 1975 actuarial cost of the pension plan was $320,000. As a result of this report, Pasther deposited $20,000 of its own money into the fund on January 12, 1976. How much should the provision for pension cost be in Pasther's 1975 income statement?
   a. $200,000
   b. $220,000
   c. $300,000
   d. $320,000

Items 6 and 7 are based on the following information:

The Track Company followed a policy of deferring all research and development costs and amortizing them over a five-year period with a full year's amortization taken in the year of the expenditure. Commencing January 1, 1975, Track changed its policy in accordance with FASB Statement of Financial Accounting Standards No. 2, to one of expensing all research and development costs as incurred. At December 31, 1974, deferred research and development costs of $3,500,000 appeared on Track's balance sheet. Research and development expenditures in 1975 amounted to $800,000.

6. What should be the amount of research and development costs charged to the income statement for the year ended December 31, 1975?
   a. $800,000.
   b. $860,000.
   c. $1,500,000.
   d. $4,300,000.

7. What should be the amount of deferred research and development costs appearing in Track's balance sheet at December 31, 1975?
   a. $0.
   b. $640,000.
   c. $2,800,000.
   d. $3,440,000.

8. The Bullet Company acquired 1,000 shares of its own common stock at $16 per share on February 5, 1974, and sold 500 of these shares at $20 per share on August 9, 1975. The market value of Bullet's common stock ws $18 per share at December 31, 1974, and the cost per share at December 31, and $21 per share at December 31, 1975. The cost method is used to record treasury stock transactions. What account(s) should Bullet credit in 1975 to record the sale of the 500 shares?
   a. Treasury stock for $10,000.
   b. Treasury stock for $8,000 and paid-in capital for $2,000.
   c. Treasury stock for $8,000 and retained earnings for $2,000.
   d. Treasury stock for $7,500 and retained earnings for $2,500.

Exhibit 2-1 (continued)

9. The Cavalier Company had 80,000 shares of treasury stock at December 31, 1974, which was acquired at $12 per share. On June 4, 1975, Cavalier issued 60,000 treasury shares to employees who exercised options under Cavalier's employee stock option plan. The market value per share was $13 at December 31, 1974, $15 at June 4, 1975, and $18 at December 31, 1975. The stock options had been granted for $11 per share. The cost method is used to record treasury stock transactions. What should be the amount of treasury stock on Cavalier's balance sheet at December 31, 1975?
   a. $ 60,000.
   b. $240,000.
   c. $300,000.
   d. $360,000.

10. On January 1, 1975, the Fulmar Company sold personal property to the Austin Company. The personal property had cost Fulmar $40,000. Fulmar frequently sells similar items of property for $44,000. Austin gave Fulmar a noninterest bearing note payable in six equal annual installments of $10,000 with the first payment due December 31, 1975. Collection of the note is reasonably assured. A reasonable rate of interest for a note of this type is 10%. The present value of an annuity of $1 in arrears at 10% for six periods is 4.355. What amount of sales revenue from this transaction should be reported in Fulmar's income statement for the year ended December 31, 1975?
    a. $10,000.
    b. $40,000.
    c. $43,550.
    d. $44,000.

11. The Mitchell Company received a seven-year non-interest bearing note on February 22, 1974, in exchange for property it sold to the Grispin Company. There was **no** established exchange price for this property and the note has **no** ready market. The prevailing rate of interest for a note of this type was 10% on February 22, 1974, 10.2% on December 31, 1974, 10.3% on February 22, 1975, and 10.4% on December 31, 1975. What interest rate should be used to calculate the interest revenue from this transaction for the year ended December 31, 1975 and 1974, respectively?
    a. 0% and 0%.
    b. 10% and 10%.
    c. 10% and 10.3%.
    d. 10.2% and 10.4%.

Items 12 and 13 are based on the following information:

On January 1, 1975, the Green Company entered into a noncancelable lease agreement with the Blatt Company for a machine which was carried on the accounting records of Green at $2,000,000. Total payments under the lease agreement which expires on December 31, 1984, aggregate $3,550,800 of which $2,400,000 represents the cost of the machine to Blatt. Payments of $335,080 are due each January 1. The first payment was made on January 1, 1975 when the lease agreement was finalized. The interest rate of 10% which was stipulated in the lease agreement is considered fair and adequate compensation to Green for the use of its funds. The "interest" method of amortization is being used. Blatt expects the machine to have a ten-year life, no salvage value, and be depreciated on a straight-line basis. The lease agreement should be accounted for as a lease equivalent to a sale by Green and as a lease which is in substance a purchase by Blatt.

Exhibit 2-1 (continued)

12. What should be the income before income taxes derived by Green from this lease for the year ended December 31, 1975?
    a. $204,492.
    b. $355,080.
    c. $604,492.
    d. $755,080.

13. **Ignoring income taxes,** what should be the expenses incurred by Blatt from this lease for the year ended December 31, 1975?
    a. $204,492.
    b. $355,080.
    c. $444,492.
    d. $595,080.

---

14. The net income for the year ended December 31, 1975, for the Kenny Company was $2,100,000. Additional information is as follows:

Capital expenditures	$6,200,000
Dividends paid on common stock	2,400,000
Dividends paid on common stock	700,000
Net increase in noncurrent deferred income tax liability	200,000
Amortization of goodwill	75,000

    Based on the information given above, what should be the working capital provided from operations in the statement of changes in financial position for the year ended December 31, 1975?
    a. $4,075,000.
    b. $4,375,000.
    c. $4,700,000
    d. $4,775,000.

15. Information concerning the debt of the Gallery Company is as follows:

    Short-term borrowings:
Balance at December 31, 1974	$ 1,200,000
Proceeds from borrowings in 1975	1,500
Payments made in 1975	(1,400,000)
Balance at December 31, 1975	$ 1,300,000

    Current portion of long-term Debt:
Balance at December 31, 1974	$ 5,500,000
Transfers from caption "Long-Term Debt"	$ 6,000,000
Payments made in 1975	(5,500,000)
Balance at December 31, 1975	$ 6,000,000)

    Long-term debt:
Balance at December 31, 1974	$42,500,000
Proceeds from borrowings in 1975	18,000,000
Transfers to caption "Current Portion of Long-Term Debt"	(6,000,000)
Payments made in 1975	(10,000,000)
Balance at December 31, 1975	$44,500,000

    Assuming funds are defined as working capital, how should the above information be shown on Gallery's statement of changes in financial position for the year ended December 31, 1975?

Exhibit 2-1 (continued)

	Source	Use
a.	$16,000,000	$18,000,000.
b.	$17,400,000	$19,500,000.
c.	$18,000,000	$16,000,000.
d.	$25,500,000	$22,900,000.

16. The stockholders' equity of the Spain Company at December 31, 1974, was as follows:

Convertible preferred stock, $20 par value. Each share convertible into 2 shares of common stock. Authorized 6,000 shares; issued and outstanding 5,000 shares	$100,000
Premium on convertible preferred stock	15,000
Common stock, $10 par value. Authorized 30,000 shares; issued and outstanding 20,000 shares	200,000
Additional paid-in capital on common stock	25,000
Retained earnings	650,000
Total stockholders' equity	$990,000

During 1975, a total of 2,000 shares of the convertible preferred stock were converted into common stock. Also during 1975, a total of 5,000 shares of common stock were issued at $15 per share. Assuming funds are defined as working capital, how should the above information be shown on Spain's statement of changes in financial position for the year ended December 31, 1975?

	Source	Use
a.	$ 46,000	$ 96,000.
b.	$ 46,000	$121,000.
c.	$121,000	$ 0.
d.	$121,000	$ 46,000.

17. At December 31, 1974, the Back Company had 350,000 shares of common stock outstanding. On September 1, 1975, an additional 150,000 shares of common stock were issued. In addition, Back had $10,000,000 of 8% convertible bonds outstanding at December 31, 1974 which are convertible into 200,000 shares of common stock. The bonds were **not** considered common stock equivalents at the time of their issuance and **no** bonds were converted into common stock in 1975. The net income for the year ended December 31, 1975, was $3,000,000. Assuming the income tax rate was 50%, what should be the fully diluted earnings per share for the year ended December 31, 1975?

a. $4.33
b. $5.00.
c. $5.67.
d. $7.50.

18. The Ackley Company Exchanged 100 shares of Burke Company common stock, which Ackley was holding as an investment, for a piece of equipment from the Flynn Company. The Burke Company common stock, which had been purchased by Ackley for $30 per share, had a quoted market value of $34 per share at the date of exchange. The piece of equipment had a recorded amount on Flynn's books of $3,100. What journal entry should Ackley have made to record this exchange?

Exhibit 2-1 (continued)

		Debit	Credit
a.	Equipment	$3,000	
	Investment in Burke Company common stock		$3,000
b.	Equipment	3,100	
	Investment in Burke Company common stock		3,000
	Other income		100
c.	Equipment	3,100	
	Other expense	300	
	Investment in Burke Company common stock		3,400
d.	Equipment	3,400	
	Investment in Burke Company common stock		3,000
	Other income		400

ANSWERS TO EXAMINATION

ACCOUNTING PRACTICE—PART I

November 3, 1976; 1:30 to 6:00 P.M.

Answer I

1. d	10. d
2. a	11. b
3. c	12. c
4. c	13. c
5. b	14. d
6. a	15. c
7. a	16. d
8. b	17. c
9. b	18. d

Uniform Certified Public Accountant Examination

(Prepared by the Board of Examiners of the American Institute of Certified Public Accountants and adopted by the examining boards of all states, territories, and the District of Columbia.)

EXAMINATION IN AUDITING

November 4, 1976; 8:30 A.M. to 12:00 M.

NOTE TO CANDIDATES: Suggested time allotments are as follows:

All questions are required.

	Estimated Minutes	
	Minimum	Maximum
No. 1	30	35
No. 2	30	35
No. 3	30	35
No. 4	15	25
No. 5	15	25
No. 6	15	25
No. 7	15	30
Total	150	210

Exhibit 2-1 (continued)

INSTRUCTIONS TO CANDIDATES

(Disregard of these instructions may be considered as indicating inefficiency in accounting work.)

1. You must arrange the papers in numerical order of the questions. If more than one page is required for an answer, write "continued" at the bottom of the page. Number pages consecutively. For instance, if 12 pages are used for your answers they should be numbered 1 through 12. The printed answer sheet provided for the objective-type items should be considered to be Page 1.

2. A CPA is continually confronted with the necessity of expressing his opinions and conclusions in written reports in clear, unequivocal language. Although the primary purpose of the examination is to test the candidate's knowledge and application of the subject matter, the ability to organize and present such knowledge in acceptable written language will be considered by the examiners.

Number 1 (Estimated time——30 to 35 minutes)
Instructions

Select the **best** answer for each of the following items. Use a soft pencil, preferably No. 2, to blacken the appropriate space on the separate printed answer sheet to indicate your answer. **Mark only one answer for each item. Answer all items.** Your grade will be based on your total correct answers.

The following is an example of the manner in which the answer sheet should be marked:

Item

96. One of the generally accepted auditing standards specifies that the auditor
    a. Inspect all fixed assets acquired during the year.
    b. Charge fair fees based on cost.
    c. Make a proper study and evaluation of the existing internal control.
    d. May not solicit clients.

Answer Sheet

96. a. ::::::::: b. ::::::::: c. ▄▄▄▄▄▄ d. :::::::::

Items to be Answered

1. A CPA would be considered "**not** associated" with unaudited financial statements when
    a. The CPA performed a limited review of a publicly-traded company's unaudited financial statements which are presented in a quarterly report to the stockholders.
    b. The CPA assisted in the preparation of the unaudited financial statements.
    c. The CPA completed an audit and rendered a report on the financial statements which without the CPA's consent were part of a prospectus which included unaudited financial statements.
    d. The CPA received all input data from the client, reviewed it, and returned it to the client for processing by an independent computer service company.

2. From which of the following evidence-gathering audit procedures would an auditor obtain **most** assurance concerning the existence of inventories?
    a. Observation of physical inventory counts.
    b. Written inventory representations from management.
    c. Confirmation of inventories in a public warehouse.
    d. Auditor's recomputation of inventory extentions.

Exhibit 2-1 (continued)

3. An important purpose of the auditor's review of the client's procurement system should be to determine the effectiveness of the procedures to protect against
    a. Improper materials handling.
    b. Unauthorized persons issuing purchase orders.
    c. Mispostings of purchase returns.
    d. Excessive shrinkage or spoilage.

4. The Auditor obtains corroborating evidential matter for accounts receivable by using positive or negative confirmation requests. Under which of the following circumstances might the negative form of the accounts receivable confirmation be useful?
    a. A substantial number of accounts are in dispute.
    b. Internal control over accounts receivable is ineffective.
    c. Client records include a large number of relatively small balances.
    d. The auditor believes that recipients of the requests are unlikely to give them consideration

5. In pursuing its quality control objectives with respect to assigning personnel to engagements, a CPA firm may use policies and procedures such as
    a. Rotating employees from assignment to assignment on a random basis to aid in the staff training effort.
    b. Requiring timely identification of the staffing requirements of specific engagements so that enough qualified personnel can be made available.
    c. Allowing staff to select the assignments of their choice to promote better client relationships.
    d. Assigning a number of employees to each engagement in excess of the number required so as **not** to overburden the staff and interfere with the quality of the audit work performed.

6. The basic concept of internal acounting control which recognizes that the cost of internal control should **not** exceed the benefits expected to be derived is known as
    a. Reasonable assurance.
    b. Management responsibility.
    c. Limited liability.
    d. Management by exception.

7. Precision is a statistical measure of the maximum likely difference between the sample estimate and the true but unknown population total, and is directly related to
    a. Reliability of evidence.
    b. Relative risk.
    c. Materiality.
    d. Cost benefit analysis.

8. Internal control over cash receipts is weakened when an employee who receives customer mail receipts also
    a. Prepares initial cash receipts records.
    b. Records credits to individual accounts receivable.
    c. Prepares bank deposit slips for all mail receipts.
    d. Maintains a petty cash fund.

9. If a company employs a capital stock registrar and/or transfer agent, the registrar or agent, or both, should be requested to confirm directly to the auditor the number of shares of each class of stock.
    a. Surrendered and canceled during the year.
    b. Authorized at the balance sheet date.
    c. Issued and outstanding at the balance sheet date.
    d. Authorized, issued and outstanding during the year.

Exhibit 2-1 (continued)

10. The primary reason why a CPA firm establishes quality control policies and procedures for professional development of staff accountants is to
    a. Comply with the continuing educational requirements imposed by various states for all staff accountants in CPA firms.
    b. Establish, in fact as well as in appearance, that staff accountants are increasing their knowledge of accounting and auditing matters.
    c. Provide a forum for staff accountants to exchange their experiences and views concerning firm policies and procedures.
    d. Provide reasonable assurance that staff personnel will have the knowledge required to enable them to fulfill their responsibilities.

11. Contact with banks for the purpose of opening company bank accounts should normally be the responsibility of the corporate
    a. Board of Directors.
    b. Treasurer.
    c. Controller.
    d. Executive Committee.

12. A company issued bonds for cash during the year under audit. To ascertain that this transaction was properly recorded, the auditor's **best** course of action is to
    a. Request a statement from the bond trustee as to the amount of the bonds issued and outstanding.
    b. Confirm the results of the issuance with the underwriter or investment banker.
    c. Trace the cash received from the issuance to the accounting records.
    d. Verify that the net cash received is credited to an account entitled "Bonds Payable."

13. The normal sequence of documents and operations on a well-prepared systems flowchart is
    a. Top to bottom and left to right.
    b. Bottom to top and left to right.
    c. Top to bottom and right to left.
    d. Bottom to top and right to left.

14. In the course of an engagement to prepare unaudited financial statements the client requests that the CPA perform normal accounts receivable audit confirmation procedures. The CPA agrees and performs such procedures. The confirmation procedures
    a. Are part of an auditing service that change the scope of the engagement to that of an audit in accordance with generally accepted auditing standards.
    b. Are part of an accounting service and are **not** performed for the purpose of conducting an audit in accordance with generally accepted auditing standards.
    c. Are **not** permitted when the purpose of the engagement is to prepare unaudited financial statements and the work to be performed is **not** in accordance with generally accepted auditing standards.
    d. Would require the CPA to render a report that indicates that the examination was conducted in accordance with generally accepted auditing standards but was limited in scope.

15. Effective internal control in a small company that has an insufficient number of employees to permit proper division of responsibilities can **best** be enhanced by
    a. Employment of temporary personnel to aid in the separation of duties.
    b. Direct participation by the owner of the business in the record-keeping activities of the business.
    c. Engaging a CPA to perform monthly "writeup" work.
    d. Delegation of full, clear-cut responsibility to each employee for the functions assigned to each.

Exhibit 2-1 (continued)

16. So that the essential accounting control features of a client's electronic data processing system can be identified and evaluated, the auditor must, at a minimum, have
    a. A basic familiarity with the computer's internal supervisory system.
    b. A sufficient understanding of the entire computer system.
    c. An expertise in computer systems analysis.
    d. A background in programming procedures.

17. Program controls, in an electronic data processing system, are used as substitutes for human controls in a manual system. Which of the following is an example of a program control?
    a. Dual read.
    b. Echo check.
    c. Validity check
    d. Limit and reasonableness test.

18. In connection with the examination of bonds payable, an auditor would expect to find in a trust indenture
    a. The issue date and maturity date of the bond.
    b. The names of the original subscribers to the bond issue.
    c. The yield to maturity of the bonds issued.
    d. The company's debt to equity ratio at the time of issuance.

19. A CPA has been engaged to audit financial statements that were prepared on a cash basis. The CPA
    a. Must ascertain that there is proper disclosure of the fact that the cash basis has been used, the general nature of material items omitted and the net effect of such omissions.
    b. May **not** be associated with such statements which are **not** in accordance with generally accepted accounting principles.
    c. Must render a qualified report explaining the departure from generally accepted accounting principles in the opinion paragraph.
    d. Must restate the financial statements on an accural basis and then render the standard (short form) report.

20. If a client is using a voucher system, the auditor who is examining accounts payable records should obtain a schedule of all unpaid vouchers at the balance sheet date and
    a. Retrace voucher register items to the source indicated in the reference column of the register.
    b. Vouch items in the voucher register and examine related canceled checks.
    c. Confirm items on the schedule of unpaid vouchers and obtain satisfaction for all confirmation exceptions.
    d. Compare the items on the schedule with open vouchers and uncanceled entries in the voucher register and account for unmatched items.

AUDITING
November 4, 1976; 8:30 A.M. to 12:00 P.M.

Answer 1

1. c	11. b
2. a	12. c
3. b	13. a
4. c	14. b
5. b	15. b
6. a	16. b
7. c	17. d
8. b	18. a
9. c	19. a
10. d	20. d

Exhibit 2-1 (continued)

Uniform Certified Public Accountant Examination

(Prepared by the Board of Examiners of the American Institute of Certified Public Accountants and adopted by the examining boards of all states, territories, and the District of Columbia.)

EXAMINATION IN BUSINESS LAW

(Commercial Law)

November 5, 1976; 8:30 A.M. to 12:00 M.

NOTE TO CANDIDATES: Suggested time allotments are as follows:

	Estimated Minutes	
All questions are required:	*Minimum*	*Maximum*
No. 1	25	30
No. 2	25	30
No. 3	25	30
No. 4	30	35
No. 5	25	30
No. 6	25	30
No. 7	20	25
Total	175	210

INSTRUCTIONS TO CANDIDATES

(Disregard of these instructions may be considered as indicating inefficiency in accounting work.)

1. You must arrange the papers in numerical order of the questions. If more than one page is required for an answer, write "continued" at the bottom of the page. Number pages consecutively. For instance, if 12 pages are used for your answers they should be numbered 1 through 12. The printed answer sheet provided for the objective-type items should be considered to be Page 1.

2. A CPA is continually confronted with the necessity of expressing his opinions and conclusions in written reports in clear, unequivocal language. Although the primary purpose of the examination is to test the candidate's knowledge and application of the subject matter, the ability to organize and present such knowledge in acceptable written language will be considered by the examiners.

Number 1 (Estimated time——25 to 30 minutes)
Instructions

Select the **best** answer for each of the following items. Use a soft pencil, preferably No. 2, to blacken the appropriate space on the separate printed answer sheet to indicate your

Exhibit 2-1 (continued)

answer. **Mark only one answer for each item. Answer all items.** Your grade will be based on your total correct answers.

The following is an example of the manner in which the answer sheet should be marked:

Item

99. The text of a letter from Bridge Builders, Inc., to Allied Steel Co. follows:

> We offer to purchase 10,000 tons of No. 4 steel pipes at today's quoted price for delivery two months from today. Your acceptance must be received in five days.

Bridge Builders intended to create a (an)
- a. Option contract.
- b. Unilateral contract.
- c. Bilateral contract.
- d. Joint contract.

Answer Sheet

99. a. ::::::::: b. ::::::::: c. ▬▬▬▬▬ d. :::::::::

Items to be Answered

1. Martin Corporation orally engaged Humm & Dawson to audit its year-end financial statements. The engagement was to be completed within two months after the close of Martin's fiscal year for a fixed fee of $2,500. Under these circumstances what obligation is assumed by Humm & Dawson?
    - a. None, because the contract is unenforceable since it is **not** in writing.
    - b. An implied promise to exercise reasonable standards of competence and care.
    - c. An implied obligation to take extraordinary steps to discover all defalcations.
    - d. The obligation of an insurer of its work which is liable without fault.

2. Which of the following can a CPA firm legally do?
    - a. Accept a competing company in the same industry as another of its clients.
    - b. Establish an association of CPAs for the purpose of determining minimum fee schedules.
    - c. Effectively disclaim liability to third parties for any and all torts.
    - d. Effectively establish an absolute dollar limitation on its liability for a given engagement.

3. Winslow Manufacturing, Inc., sought a $200,000 loan from National Lending Corporation. National Lending insisted that audited financial statements be submitted before it would extend credit. Winslow agreed to this and also agreed to pay the audit fee. An audit was performed by an independent CPA who submitted his report to Winslow to be used solely for the purpose of negotiating a loan from National. National, upon reviewing the audited financial statements, decided in good faith **not** to extend the credit desired. Certain ratios, which as a matter of policy were used by National in reaching its decision, were deemed too low. Winslow used copies of the audited financial statements to obtain credit elsewhere. It was subsequently learned that the CPA, despite the exercise of reasonable care, had failed to discover a sophisticated embezzlement scheme by Winslow's chief accountant. Under these circumstances, what liability does the CPA have?
    - a. The CPA is liable to third parties who extended credit to Winslow based upon the audited financial statements.
    - b. The CPA is liable to Winslow to repay the audit fee because credit was **not** extended by National.
    - c. The CPA is liable to Winslow for any losses Winslow suffered as a result of failure to discover the embezzlement.
    - d. The CPA is **not** liable to any of the parties.

Exhibit 2-1 (continued)

4. An investor seeking to recover stock market losses from a CPA firm, based upon an unqualified opinion on financial statements which accompanied a registration statement must establish that
   a. There was a false statement or omission of material fact contained in the audited financial statements.
   b. He relied upon the financial statements.
   c. The CPA firm did **not** act in good faith.
   d. The CPA firm would have discovered the false statement or omission if it had exercised due care in its examination.

5. Under what conditions will the statute of frauds be a defense under the Uniform Commercial Code where there is a contract for the sale of goods worth more than $500?
   a. The seller has completed goods specially manufactured for the buyer which are **not** salable in the ordinary course of the seller's business.
   b. The written memorandum omits several important terms but states the quanity, and it is signed by the party to be charged.
   c. The party asserting the statute of frauds admits under oath to having made the contract.
   d. The goods in question are fungible and actively traded by merchants in the business community.

6. Walker and White entered into a written contract involving the purchase of certain used equipment by White. White claims that there were oral understandings between the parties which are included as a part of the contract. Walker pleads the parol evidence rule. This rule applies to
   a. Subsequent oral modifications of the written contract by the parties.
   b. Additional consistent terms even if the contract was **not** intended as a complete and exclusive listing of all terms of the agreement.
   c. A contemporaneous oral understanding of the parties which contradicts the terms of a written contract intended as the final expression of the agreement between the parties.
   d. Evidence in suport of the oral modification based upon the performance by Walker.

7. If a seller repudiates his contract for the sale of 100 radios with a buyer, what recourse does the buyer have?
   a. He can "cover," i.e., procure the goods elsewhere and recover the difference.
   b. He can obtain specific performance by the seller.
   c. He can recover punitive damages.
   d. He must await the sellers performance for a commercially reasonable time after the repudiation.

8. Berg is the founder and senior partner of Berg Associates, a consulting firm. He is now 75 years old and wants to retire. The other partners have agreed to purchase Berg's partnership **interest for $250,000; the amount includes** $50,000 for goodwill. The agreement also provides for the right of the other partners to continue the business and the right to use Berg's name. Berg is to receive $100,000 **upon his retirement and an additional** $50,000 per year for three years. The remaining partners agreed to hold Berg **harmless** for any past or future debts of the partnership and release him from all liability. If Berg accepts this offer to sell his partnership interest, it means that
   a. The existing firm (Berg Associates) has **not** been dissolved because the business is to be carried on by the remaining partners.
   b. The remaining partners may **not** use the original firm name, but may only indicate **the newly named firm formerly was known as "Berg Associates."**

Exhibit 2-1 (continued)

    c. The payment of $50,000 for the goodwill of Berg has important tax consequences to him and the firm.
    d. Berg as a retired partner has the right to attend and vote in the year-end partnership meeting.

9. Kent, a wholesale distributor of cameras, entered into a contract with Williams. Williams agreed to purchase 100 cameras with certain optional **attachments**. The contract was made on October 1, 1976, for delivery by October 15, 1976; terms: 2/10, net 30. Kent shipped the cameras on October 6, and they were delivered on October 10. The shipment did **not** conform to the contract, in that one of the attachments was **not** included. Williams immediately notified Kent that he was rejecting the goods. For maximum legal advantage Kent's most appropriate action is to
    a. Bring an action for the price less an allowance for the missing attachment.
    b. Notify Williams promptly of his intention to cure the defect and make a conforming delivery by October 15.
    c. Terminate his contract with Williams and recover for breach of contract.
    d. Sue Williams for specific performance.

10. Grand, a general partner, retired, and the partnership held a testimonial dinner for him and invited ten of the partnership's largest customers to attend. A week later a notice was placed in various trade journals indicating that Grand had retired and was no longer associated with the partnership in any capacity. After the appropriate public notice of Grand's retirement, which of the following **best** describes his legal status?
    a. The release of Grand by the remaining partners and the assumption of all past and future debts of the partnership by them via a "hold harmless" clause constitutes a novation.
    b. Grand has the apparent authority to bind the partnership in contracts he makes with persons who have previously dealt with the partnership and are unaware of his retirement.
    c. Grand has **no** liability to past creditors upon his retirement from the partnership if they all have been informed of his withdrawal and his release from liability, and if they do **not** object within 60 days.
    d. Grand has the legal status of a limited partner for the three years it takes to pay him the balance of the purchase price of his partnership interest.

11. A limited partner
    a. May **not** withdraw his capital contribution unless there is sufficient limited-partnership property to pay all general creditors.
    b. Must **not** own limited-partnership interests in other competing limited partnerships.
    c. Is automatically an agent for the partnership with apparent authority to bind the limited partership in contract.
    d. Has **no** liability to creditors even if he takes part in the control of the business as long as he is held out as being a limited partner.

12. Martin, a wholesale distributor, made a contract for the purchase of 10,000 gallons of gasoline from the Wilberforce Oil Company. The price was to be determined in accordance with the refinery price as of the close of business on the delivery date. Credit terms were net/30 after delivery. Under these circumstances which of the following statements is true?
    a. If Martin pays upon delivery, he is entitled to a 2% discount.
    b. The contract being silent on the place of delivery, Martin has the right to expect delivery at his place of business.
    c. Although the price has some degree of uncertainty, the contract is enforceable.
    d. Because the goods involved are tangible, specific performance is a remedy available to Martin.

Exhibit 2-1 (continued)

13. Absent any contrary provisions in the agreement, under which of the following circumstances will a limited partnership be dissolved?
    a. A limited partner dies and his estate is insolvent.
    b. A personal creditor of a general partner obtains judgement against the general partner's interest in the limited partnership.
    c. A general partner retires and all the remaining general partners do **not** consent to continue.
    d. A limited partner assigns his partnership interest to an outsider and the purchaser becomes a substituted limited partner.

14. A valid limited partnership
    a. Created pursuant to state law **cannot** be treated as an "association" for federal income tax purposes.
    b. **Cannot** be created unless there is an enabling statute in the jurisdiction.
    c. Is exempt from all Securities and Exchange Commission regulations.
    d. Must designate in its certificate the name, residence, and capital contribution of each general partner but need **not** include this information in respect to limited partners.

15. A limited partner's capital contribution to the limited partnership
    a. Creates an intangible personal property right of the limited partner in the limited partnership.
    b. Can be withdrawn at the limited partner's option at any time prior to the filing of a petition in bankruptcy against the limited partnership.
    c. Can only consist of cash or marketable securities.
    d. Need **not** be indicated in the limited partnership's certificte.

16. **Bonanza Real Estate Ventures** is a limited partnership created pursuant to the law of a state which has adopted the Uniform Limited Partnership Act. It has three general partners and 1,100 limited partners living in various states. The limited-partnership interests were offered to the general public at $5,000 per partnership interest. Under these circumstances which of the following statements is true?
    a. The general partners must contribute capital of at least $5,000 each.
    b. The general partners have unlimited liability; thus, they **cannot** purchase a limited-partnerships interest also.
    c. The limited-partnership interests are "securities" within the meaning of the Securities Act of 1933.
    d. The limited-partnership interest **cannot** be sold in any state which has **not** adopted the Uniform Limited Partnership Act.

Answer 1

1. b
2. a
3. d
4. a
5. d
6. c
7. a
8. c
9. b
10. b
11. a
12. c
13. c
14. b
15. a
16. c

Exhibit 2-1 (continued)

Uniform Certified Public Accountant Examination

(Prepared by the Board of Examiners of the American Institute of Certified Public Accountants and adopted by the examining boards of all states, territories, and the District of Columbia.)

EXAMINATION IN ACCOUNTING THEORY

(Theory of Accounts)

November 5, 1976; 1:30 to 5:00 P.M.

NOTE TO CANDIDATES: Suggested time allotments are as follows:

All questions are required:	Estimated Minutes Minimum	Maximum
No. 1	35	40
No. 2	35	40
No. 3	20	25
No. 4	20	30
No. 5	20	25
No. 6	15	20
No. 7	20	30
Total	165	210

INSTRUCTIONS TO CANDIDATES

(Disregard of these instructions may be considered as indicating inefficiency in accounting work.)

1. You must arrange the papers in numerical order of the questions. If more than one page is required for an answer, write "continued" at the bottom of the page. Number pages consecutively. For instance, if 12 pages are used for your answers they should be numbered 1 through 12. The printed answer sheet provided for the objective-type items should be considered to be Page 1.

2. A CPA is continually confronted with the necessity of expressing his opinions and conclusions in written reports in clear, unequivocal language. Although the primary purpose of the examination is to test the candidate's knowledge and application of the subject matter, the ability to organize and present such knowledge in acceptable written language will be considered by the examiners.

Exhibit 2-1 (continued)

Number 1 (Estimated time — —35 to 40 minutes)

Instructions

Select the **best** answer for each of the following items relating to **a variety of issues in financial accounting, Opinions of the Accounting Principles Board, and Statements of the Financial Accounting Standards Board.** Use a soft pencil, preferably No. 2, to blacken the appropriate space on the separate printed answer sheet to indicate your answer. **Mark only one answer for each item. Answer all items.** Your grade will be based on your total correct answers.

The following is an example of the manner in which the answer sheet should be marked:

Item

99. The recommended title for the financial statement which summarizes changes in financial position is the statement of
   a. Changes in financial position.
   b. Changes in working capital.
   c. Sources and applications of funds.
   d. Cash flow.

Answer Sheet

99. a. ■■■■■ b. :::::::: c. :::::::: d. ::::::::

Items to be Answered

1. Depreciation measurement should be based on
   a. Past input exchange price.
   b. Current input exchange price.
   c. Future input exchange price.
   d. Current output exchange price.

2. Which of the following methods of determining annual bad debt expense **best** achieves the matching concept?
   a. Percentage of sales.
   b. Percentage of ending accounts receivable.
   c. Percentage of average accounts receivable.
   d. Direct write-off.

3. Revenue is generally recognized when the earning process is virtually complete and an exchange has taken place. What principle is described herein?
   a. Consistency.
   b. Matching.
   c. Realization.
   d. Conservatism.

4. Which type of accounting change should always be accounted for in current and future periods?
   a. Change in accounting principle.
   b. Change in reporting entity.
   c. Change in accounting estimate.
   d. Correction of an error.

Exhibit 2-1 (continued)

5. The Raider Company changed its method of pricing inventories from first-in, first-out to last-in, first-out. What type of accounting change does this represent?
    a. A change in accounting estimate for which the financial statements for the prior periods included for comparative purposes should be presented as previously reported.
    b. A change in accounting principle for which the financial statements for prior periods included for comparative purposes should be presented as previously reported.
    c. A change in accounting estimate for which the financial statements for prior periods included for comparative purposes should be restated.
    d. A change in accounting principle for which the financial statements for prior periods included for comparative purposes should be restated.

6. A company has four "deferred income tax" accounts arising from timing differences involving: (1) current assets, (2) noncurrent assets, (3) current liabilities, and (4) noncurrent liabilities. The presentation of these four "deferred income tax" accounts in the statement of financial position should be shown as
    a. A single net amount.
    b. A net current and a net noncurrent amount.
    c. Four accounts with **no** netting permitted.
    d. Valuation adjustments of the related assets and liabilities that gave rise to the deferred tax.

7. Which of the following situations would require use of interperiod tax allocation procedures?
    a. Research and development costs are deducted for income tax purposes in the year incurred.
    b. A material gain on a sale-leaseback transaction is taxed in the year of sale.
    c. Unamortized discount and call premium on an early extinguishment of debt are deducted for income tax purposes in the year of extinguishment.
    d. The amount of a material loss on the sale of an asset differs for tax and accounting purposes because of different bases for this asset. The different bases are due to a quasi-reorganization recognized for accounting but **not** for income tax purposes.

8. What theory of ownership equity is enumerated by the following equation: assets minus liabilities minus preferred stock equity equals common stock equity?
    a. Fund.
    b. Enterprise.
    c. Entity.
    d. Residual equity.

9. Companies A and B have been operating separately for five years. Each company has a minimal amount of liabilities and a simple capital structure consisting solely of voting common stock. Company A, in exchange for 40 percent of its voting stock, acquires 80 percent of the common stock of Company B. This was a "tax free" stock for stock (type B) exchange for tax purposes. Company B assets have a total net fair market value of $800,000 and a total net book value of $580,000. The fair market value of the A stock used in the exchange was $700,000. The goodwill on this acquisition would be
    a. Zero, this would be a pooling of interest.
    b. $60,000.
    c. $120,000.
    d. $236,000.

Exhibit 2-1 (continued)

10. Drab, Inc., owns 40% of the outstanding stock of the Gloom Company. During 1975, Drab received a $4,000 cash dividend from Gloom. What effect did this dividend have on Drab's 1975 financial statements?
    a. Increased total assets.
    b. Decreased total assets.
    c. Increased income.
    d. Decreased investment account.

11. When preparing combined or consolidated financial statements for a domestic and a foreign company, the account balances expressed in the foreign currency must be translated into the domestic currency. The objective of the translation process is to obtain currency valuations that
    a. Are conservative.
    b. Reflect current monetary equivalents.
    c. Are expressed in domestic units of measure and are in conformity with domestic generally accepted accounting principles.
    d. Reflect the translated account at its unexpired historical cost.

---

12. How should cumulative preferred dividends in arrears be shown in a corporation's statement of financial position?
    a. Footnote.
    b. Increase in stockholders' equity.
    c. Increase in current liabilities.
    d. Increase in current liabilities for the amount expected to be declared within the year operating cycle, and increase in long-term liabilities for the balance.

13. Milner Company issued what is called a "100% stock dividend" on its common stock. Milner did **not** change the par value of the common stock. At what amount per share, if any, should either paid-in capital or retained earnings be reduced for this transaction?
    a. Zero because no entry is made.
    b. Par value.
    c. Market value at the declaration date.
    d. Market value at the date of issuance.

14. A graph is set up with "depreciation expense" on the vertical axis and "time" on the horizontal axis. Assuming linear relationships, how would the graphs for straight-line and sum-of-the-years'-digits depreciation, respectively, be drawn?
    a. Vertically and sloping down to the right.
    b. Vertically and sloping up to the right.
    c. Horizontally and sloping down to the right.
    d. Horizontally and sloping up to the right.

15. At the beginning of 1973, Garmar Company received a three-year noninterest-bearing $1,000 trade note. The market rate for equivalent notes was 8% at that time. Garmar reported this note as $1,000 trade notes receivable on its 1973 year-end statement of financial position and $1,000 as sales revenue for 1973. What effect did this accounting for the note have on Garmar's net earnings for 1973, 1974, and 1975, and its retained earnings at the **end** of 1975, respectively?
    a. Overstate, understate, understate, zero.
    b. Overstate, understate, understate, understate.
    c. Overstate, overstate, understate, zero.
    d. **No** effect on any of these.

Exhibit 2-1 (continued)

16. Which of the following items represents a potential use of working capital?
    a. Goodwill amortization.
    b. Sale of fixed assets at a loss.
    c. Net loss from operations.
    d. Declaration of a stock dividend.

17. When a company adopts a pension plan for accounting purposes, past service costs should be
    a. Treated as a prior period adjustment because **no** future periods are benefitted.
    b. Amortized in accordance with procedures used for income tax purposes.
    c. Amortized under accrual accounting to current and future periods benefitted.
    d. Treated as an expense of the period during which the funding occurs.

18. In considering interim financial reporting, how did the Accounting Principles Board conclude that such reporting should be viewed?
    a. As a "special" type of reporting that need **not** follow generally accepted accounting principles.
    b. As useful only if activity is evenly spread throughout the year so that estimates are unnecessary.
    c. As reporting for a basic accounting period.
    d. As reporting for an integral part of an annual period.

Items 19 through 22 are based on the following instructions:

Each item describes an **independent** situation. For each situation, one factor is denoted X and the other factor is denoted Y. For each situation, compare the two factors to determine whether X is greater than, equal to, or less than Y.

19. Delta Corporation wrote off a $100 uncollectible account receivable against the $1,200 balance in its allowance account. Compare the current ratio **before** the write off (X) with the current ratio **after** the write off (Y).
    a. X greater than Y.
    b. X equals Y.
    c. X less than Y.
    d. Cannot be determined.

20. Kappa, Inc., neglected to amortize the premium on its bonds payable. Compare the company's net earnings **without** this premium amortization (X) and the company's net earnings with such amortization (Y).
    a. X greater than Y.
    b. X equals Y.
    c. X less than Y.
    d. Cannot be determined.

21. Aaron, Inc., owns 80% of the outstanding stock of Belle, Inc. Compare the consolidated net earnings of Aaron and Belle (X) and Aaron's net earnings if it does **not** consolidate with Belle (Y).
    a. X greater than Y.
    b. X equals Y.
    c. X less than Y.
    d. Cannot be determined.

Exhibit 2-1 (continued)

22. Epsilon Company has a current ratio of 2 to 1. A transaction reduces the current ratio. Compare the working capital **before** this transaction (X) and the working capital **after** this transaction (Y).
   a. X greater than Y.
   b. X equals Y.
   c. X less than Y.
   d. Cannot be determined.

Number 3 (Estimated time——20 to 25 minutes)

Financial accounting usually emphasizes the economic substance of events even though the legal form may differ and suggest different treatment. For example, under accrual accounting, expenses are recognized when they are incurred (substance) rather than when cash is disbursed (form).

Although the feature of substance over form exists in most generally accepted accounting principles and practices, there are times when form prevails over substance.

Required:
For each of the following topics, discuss the underlying theory in terms of both substance and form, i.e., substance over form and possibly form over substance in some cases. Each topic should be discussed independently.
   a. Consolidated financial statements.
   b. Equity method of accounting for investments in common stock.
   c. Leases (including sale and leaseback.)
   d. Earnings per share (complex capital structure).

ACCOUNTING THEORY

(Theory of Accounts)

November 5, 1976; 1:30 to 5:00 P.M.

Answer 1
1. a
2. a
3. c
4. c
5. b
6. b
7. b
8. d
9. b
10. d
11. c
12. a
13. b
14. c
15. a
16. c
17. c
18. d
19. b
20. c
21. b
22. d

Exhibit 2-1 (continued)

a. The theory underlying consolidated financial statements is that two or more legally separate entities are treated as one economic unit. In form they are distinct conpanies, but, in substance, they are viewed as one because of the control exercised by the parent company and other factors. The purpose of consolidated financial statements is to reflect transactions between the consolidated entity and outside parties, such as customers. Therefore, transactions among the related companies (intercompany transactions) do not affect the final statements.

To issue consolidated financial statements, the parent company must control the subsidiary companies. Control, in this sense, is defined as owning more than 50% of the voting stock. While this is the form of control, the substance must also be considered. If the two conflict, substance must prevail. In other words, factors in addition to control must be considered before consolidated financial statements can validly be issued. The factors include the following: the expectation of continuity of control; the degree of existing restrictions upon the availability of assets and earnings of a subsidiary; the general coincidence of accounting periods; the degree of homogeneity in the assets and operations of the other companies (although the importance of this is reduced by segment reporting); and whether control is operational or not. If these conditions do not appear to warrant consolidated financial statements, such statements should not be issued even though the form of control—more than 50% ownership—exists.

A company may own less than 50% of another company and still exercise control in substance. In this case, though, form is accorded greater weight than substance because consolidated financial statements would not be permitted. This situation illustrates the recognition of form over substance.

b. The equity method of accounting for investments in common stock involves increasing or decreasing the investment account for the investor's share of the investee's reported earnings or losses (after adjustment for intercompany profits) and decreasing the investment account when the investor receives dividends from the investee. The investor's earnings, therefore, are increased by the investee's reported earnings for the period (substance), whether or not these earnings are actually distributed by the investee (form). In other words, substance is recognized over form for reporting an investor's share of an investee's earnings.

The equity method is assumed to be appropriate if an investor can influence the operating or financial decisions of the investee. In form, such influence implies ownership of more than 50% of the voting stock of the investee. In substance, though, such influence can be present even if the stock ownership in the investee is less than 50%. Again, substance prevails over form because the equity method of acounting for the investment is required when an investor owns at least 20% of the voting stock of an investee, unless there is evidence that the investor cannot exercise significant influence over the investee.

c. Leases that are equivalent to an installment purchase of the property must be recorded as such on the books of the lessee, who is assumed, in substance, to be acquiring property. The property and related obligation (liability) initially must be included in the lessee's statement of financial position at the discounted amount of the future rents and other payments. The lessee would then charge interest expense and depreciation expense each year instead of rent expense. In form, this is a lease agreement; in substance, it is equivalent to a purchase because certain criteria are met. In the absence of these established criteria, the lease is treated as an operating lease with no capitalization required and rent expense charged annually. In this latter case, the aggreement is a lease in form and substance.

This decision on whether or not to record the acquisition of an asset and incurrence of a liability is based on the substance of what the lessee is assumed to be acquiring. If the lessee is assumed to be acquiring equity in the asset, the lease should be

Exhibit 2-1 (continued)

considered a purchase. If the lessee is assumed to be acquiring current service value of the asset, the lease should not be considered a purchase.

Accounting for leases by lessors is also governed by the feature of substance over form. The lessor may be investing in property and leasing the property to earn a return on the investment (financial institution), or may be leasing property to facilitate the sale or use of its own manufactured product (manufacturer or dealer lessor), or may be leasing the property for profit (leasing company). The first two reasons cited above for leasing usually meet specified criteria to treat the lease as a financing lease if the lessor is a financial institution or a sale if the lessor is a manufacturer or dealer. Although these criteria are not exactly the same, they both view the substance as not being an operating lease. In substance, the financial institution is assumed to hold a receivable rather than the property leased; the manufacturer or dealer is assumed to have sold the property leased. Again the discounted value of the future rental receipts must be used to set up the receivable or reflect the sale. If the lessor is assumed to be leasing property for profit, the lease is treated as such in substance as well as form; that is, it is assumed to be an operating lease.

Leases can be viewed as a specific example of long-term noncancelable commitments. Such commitments other than leases do not have to be capitalized even though many of them, in substance, represent an acquisition of an asset and incurrence of the related liability. In this case, form prevails over substance.

Sometimes the owner of property sells the property to another parrty and simultaneously leases it back. Although the sale and lease are legally distinct, this sale-and-leaseback transaction is, in substance, a single transaction, a borrowing and secured transaction, and should be accounted for as such. Any material gain or loss on the sale of the property should be amortized over the lease rather than be recognized immediately.

d. The theory underlying required earnings-per-share calculations is that various securities (convertible securities, options, and warrants) that are not common stock in form may be treated as equivalent to common stock in substance if certain specified conditions prevail. The concept that a security may be the equivalent of common stock has evolved to meet the reporting needs of investors in corporations that have issued certain types of convertible and other complex securities. A common stock equivalent is a security which is not, in form, common stock, but which contains provisions to enable its holder to become a common stockholder and which, because of the terms and the circumstances under which it was issued, is in substance equivalent to a common stock. Neither conversion or exercise, nor the imminence of conversion or exercise is necessary to cause a security to be a common stock equivalent, but the existence of the option to convert is essential.

Once the definition has been established for a common stock equivalent, all convertible bonds and convertible preferred stock appear to be common stock equivalents in form. Again, though, substance prevails because a test must be met to determine this status. To be a comon stock equivalent, at issuance the security must have a cash yield that is less than 66-2/3% of the then current bank prime interest rate. Although this criterion is somewhat arbitrary, it is an attempt to estimate a comparable rate for a similar security of the issuer with no conversion option. In other words, it is an attempt to add substance to the definition used for a common stock equivalent. Because of the "only at issuance" measurement date, this can also result in form over substance—that is, subsequent events could make other securities the equivalent of common stock even though they failed the test at issuance.

The earnings-per-share calculations must be shown on the bottom of a company's earnings statement. The financial statements of a company are historical in nature, and, therefore, one might expect that earnings-per-share calculations are historical in form because they appear on these historical financial statements. In substance, though, the earnings-per-share calculations are pro forma because they are based on assumed conversion of securities and assumed exercise of options.

Exhibit 2-1 (continued)

> Although the inherent theory underlying earnings-per-share calculations relies on substance over form, there are specific instances where form prevails over substance. Convertible securities (bonds and preferred stock) are treated differently from securities with detachable warrants. The convertible securities are classified as common stock equivalents based on the facts when they are issued; the warrants are classified according to conditions at each period. These securities are different in form but similar in substance because the proceeds from the exercise of the warrants can be used to purchase the original bond or preferred stock leaving the firm in the same position as when convertible securities are converted.

213 How to Prepare to Take the CPA Examination

The CPA examination is a three-day task beginning at 1:30 p.m. on Wednesday afternoon and ending at 5:00 p.m. on Friday. A candidate who has devoted a sufficient period of time in preparation and is accustomed to taking examinations should be able to perform in a satisfactory manner. The preparation includes completing the courses prescribed by the state board and reviewing the course material shortly prior to sitting for the CPA examination. The candidate will be the best judge as to the adequacy of his preparation. Completion of the course work and a review of textbooks and class notes may be adequate for some candidates who did well in school and who can exercise control of their study habits. For those who are not quite so fortunate, a more rigorous program may be required.

For additional preparation to sit for the CPA examination, the candidate may select other means such as CPA review courses sponsored by a college or university or a private CPA preparatory course. The cost would probably range from about $250 to $500. Review courses usually are held during the three- or four-month period preceding the May and November examinations. The state societies of CPAs and the local firms and universities will be aware of programs in your area.

Material and means available for use in the CPA review include

1. Your textbooks and class notes
2. Previous CPA examinations and sample solutions
3. CPA review manuals and solutions, such as:
    a. John W. Anderson and Robert W. Lentilhon, *The CPA Examination: Volume I—Practice, Auditing, and Theory* (Cincinnati: South-Western, 1972).
    b. Charles T. Horngren and L. Arthur Leer, *CPA Problems and Approaches,* 4th ed. (Englewood Cliffs, N.J.: Prentice-Hall, 1974).
    c. Thomas D. Hubbard, Larry N. Killough, and Ronald J. Patten, *CPA Review: Theory, Auditing, Law* (New York: Wiley & Sons, 1974).

d. Harold Q. Langenderfer and E. Ben Yager, *CPA Examination — A Comrehensive Review,* 2nd ed. (Columbus, Oh.: Charles E. Merrill, 1974).
   e. Herbert E. Miller and George C. Mead, *CPA Review Manual,* 4th ed. (Englewood Cliffs, N.J.: Prentice-Hall, 1972).
   f. George C. Thompson and Gerald P. Brady, *Shortened CPA Law Review,* 3rd ed. (Belmont, Ca.: Wadsworth, 1971).
4. CPA review courses:
   a. College or university sponsored.
   b. Private review courses, such as:*

   Becker, CPA Review Course
   15760 Ventura Blvd., 11th Floor
   Encino, California 91436

   Jerrell Sims CPA Review Course
   511 North Akard St.
   Suite A
   Dallas, Texas 75201

The accountant who is employed by a public accounting firm is expected to obtain a CPA certificate as soon as possible. Those who work for the government of private industry may not be expected to obtain a certificate; however, the time and effort devoted in this direction will probably force the person to be a better professional, and the possibilities of a promotion will certainly be advanced.

220 THE CERTIFICATE IN MANAGEMENT ACCOUNTING EXAM

The Certificate in Management Accounting (CMA) examination is offered nationwide each June by the Institute of Management Accounting of the National Association of Accountants. The intent of the CMA exam is to provide evidence of proficiency in various areas of management accounting, including periodic reporting and decision analysis. The exam is part of an overall CMA program initiated in order to establish management accounting as a recognized profession.

Administered over a two-and-a-half day period, the exam consists of five parts:

Wednesday

Part 1 1:30 - 5:00 p.m.   Economics and Business Finance

Thursday

Part 2 8:30 -12:00   Organization and Behavior, Including Ethical Considerations

*Other courses are often advertised in the *Journal of Accountancy.*

Part 3   1:30 - 5:00 p.m.   Public Reporting Standards,
                                 Auditing and Taxes

Friday

Part 4   8:30 -12:00   Periodic Reporting for
                                 Internal and External
                                 Purposes

Part 5   1:30 - 5:00 p.m.   Decision Analysis, Including
                                 Modeling and Information
                                 Systems

Copies of recent exams, including unofficial answers to all parts, are available in booklet form for a small fee from the National Association of Accountants (NAA). Requests should be mailed to:

> Special Order Department
> National Association of Accountants
> 919 Third Avenue
> New York, New York 10022.

In the past the NAA has published the exam in parts, along with the unofficial answers, in its monthly publication, *Management Accounting*.

Additional information about the CMA exam, including upcoming exam dates and location cities, can be obtained from:

> Institute of Management Accounting
> 570 City Center Building
> Ann Arbor, Michigan 48108.

221   Sample CMA Exam

A sample instruction sheet and five questions from the December 1974 CMA exam are shown in Exhibit 2-2. Although the instruction sheet is from Part 5 of the exam, it — as well as the questions that follow — is representative of the exam as a whole.

Exhibit 2-2
Sample CMA Exam

Management Accounting Examination

Examination for the Certificate in Management Accounting Program given by the Institute of Management Accounting (570 City Center Building, Ann Arbor, Michigan 48108), of the National Association of Accountants (919 Third Avenue, New York, New York 10022).

Exhibit 2-2 (continued)

Examination for Part 5

Decision Analysis, Including Modeling and Information Systems

Friday, December 6, 1974; 1:30 p.m. to 5:00 p.m.

	Estimated Time
Section A (All Questions are Required)	
Number 1	½ hour
Number 2	½ hour
Number 3	½ hour
Number 4	½ hour
Section B (A set of common data provides the basis for all questions in this section. All questions are required.)	
Number 5, Number 6, and Number 7	1½ hours
	3½ hours

The time allowance suggested approximates the relative weight assigned each question.

INSTRUCTIONS TO CANDIDATES

1. Place your candidate number at the top of each answer sheet you submit. Begin each question on a new sheet of paper. Arrange your answers in the numerical order of the problems. Number all pages in order.
2. Calculations made to support your answers to problem and analysis questions should be legible and clearly referenced to your answers.
3. Answers to questions should be well written. Illegible writing and lack of clear exposition will influence the evaluation of the examiners.

FAILURE TO FOLLOW THESE INSTRUCTIONS MAY RESULT IN FAILURE OF WHAT OTHERWISE MIGHT HAVE BEEN PASSING WORK.

Note: Material from the Certificate in Management Accounting Examinations, Copyright © 1974 by the National Association of Accountants, is reprinted with permission.

PART 1

QUESTION NUMBER 6 (An Alternate to Number 7)—Estimated time ½ hour

The treasurer of a new venture, Start-Up Scientific, Inc., is trying to determine how to raise $6,000,000 of long-term capital. His investment adviser has devised the alternative capital structures shown below:

Exhibit 2-2 (continued)

Alternative A

$2,000,000   9% Debt
$4,000,000   Equity

If this alternative is chosen, the firm would sell 200,000 shares of common stock to net $20 per share. Stockholders would expect an initial dividend of $1.00 per share and a dividend growth rate of 7 percent.

Alternative B

$4,000,000   12% Debt
$2,000,000   Equity

Under this alternative, the firm would sell 100,000 shares of common stock to net $20 per share. The expected initial dividend would be $0.90 per share, and the anticipated dividend growth rate is 12 percent.

Assume that the firm earns a profit under either capital structure and that the effective tax rate is 50 percent.

Required:

A. What is the cost of capital to the firm under each of the suggested capital structures? Explain your result.

B. Explain the logic of the anticipated higher interest rate on debt associated with Alternative B.

C. Is it logical for shareholders to expect a higher dividend growth rate under Alternative B? Explain your answer.

PART 2

QUESTION NUMBER 5—Estimated time ½ hour

Duval, Inc. is a large publicly held corporation that is well known throughout the United States for its product. The corporation has always had good profit margins and excellent earnings. However, Duval has experienced a leveling of sales and a reduced market share in the past two years resulting in a stabilization of profits rather than growth. Despite these trends, the firm has maintained an excellent cash and short-term investment position. The president has called a meeting of the treasurer and the vice presidents for sales and production to develop alternative strategies for improving Duval's performance. The four individuals form the nucleus of a well organized management team that has worked together for several years to bring success to Duval, Inc.

The sales vice president suggests that sales levels can be improved by presenting the company's product in a more attractive and appealing package. He also recommends that advertising be increased, and that the current price be maintained. This latter step would have the effect of a price decrease because the prices of most other competing products are rising.

The treasurer is skeptical of maintaining the present price when others are increasing prices since this will curtail revenues, unless this policy provides a competitive advantage. He also points out that the repackaging will increase costs in the near future, at least, because of the start-up costs of a new packing process. He does not favor increasing advertising outright because he is doubtful of the short-run benefit.

Exhibit 2-2 (continued)

The sales vice president replies that increased, or at least redirected, advertising is necessary to promote the price stability and to take advantage of the new packaging; the combination would provide the company with a competitive advantage. The president adds that the advertising should be studied closely to determine the type of advertising to be used—television, radio, newspaper, magazine. In addition if television is used, attention must be directed to the type of programs to be sponsored—children's, family, sporting events, news specials, etc.

The production vice president suggests several possible production improvements, such as a systems study of the manufacturing process to identify changes in the work-flow which would cut costs. He suggests operating costs could be further reduced by the purchase of new equipment. The product could be improved by employing a better grade of raw materials and by engineering changes in the fabrication of the product. When queried by the president on the impact of the proposed changes, the production vice president indicated that the primary benefit would be product performance, but that appearance and safety would also be improved. The sales vice president and treasurer commented that this would result in increased sales.

The treasurer notes that all of the production proposals would increase immediate costs, and this could result in lower profits. If profit performance is going to be improved, the price structure should be examined closely. He recommends that the current level of capital expenditures be maintained unless substantial cost savings can be obtained.

The treasurer further believes that expenditures for research and development should be decreased since previous outlays have not prevented a decrease in Duval's share of the market. The production vice president agrees that the research and development activities have not proven profitable, but thinks that this is because the research effort was applied in the wrong area. The sales vice president cautions against any drastic reductions because the packaging change will only provide a temporary advantage in the market; consequently, more effort will have to be devoted to product development.

Focusing on the use of liquid assets and the present high yields on securities, the treasurer suggests that the firm's profitability can be improved by shifting funds from the presently held short-term marketable securities to longer term, higher yield securities. He further states that cost reductions would provide more funds for investments. He recognizes that the restructuring of the investments from short-term to long-term would hamper flexibility.

In his summarizing comments, the president observes that they have a good start and the ideas provide some excellent alternatives. He states, "I think we ought to develop these ideas further and consider other ramifications. For instance, what effect would new equipment and the systems study have on the labor force? Shouldn't we also consider the environmental impact of any plant and product change? We want to appear as a leader in our industry—not a follower.

"I note that none of you considered increased community involvement through such groups as the Chamber of Commerce and the United Fund.

"The factors you mentioned plus those additional points all should be considered as we reach a decision on the final course of action we will follow."

Required:

A. State explicitly the implied corporate goals being expressed by each of the following:
   1. Treasurer.
   2. Sales vice president.
   3. Production vice president.
   4. President.

Exhibit 2-2 (continued)

B. Compare the type of goals discussed above with the corporate goal(s) postulated by the economic theory of the firm.

PART 3

QUESTION NUMBER 1—Estimated Time 1 hour

INSTRUCTIONS: Select the BEST answer for each of the items below. Your answer is to be marked on the answer sheet provided. Mark your answer by blackening the appropriate answer space with a soft lead pencil. Mark ONLY ONE ANSWER for each item. Your grade will be determined from your total of correct answers.

Sample Item:

101. Which of the following outlays is **not** a potential deduction from income for the computation of taxable income?
    a. Contribution to the Boy Scouts.
    b. Payment of property taxes.
    c. Payment of federal income taxes.
    d. Payment of bond interest charges.
    e. Payment of building rental charge.

Answer Sheet

101. a.:::::::::: b.:::::::::: c.■■■■■■ d.:::::::::: e.::::::::::

Answer the Following Items:

1. When a corporation incurs state income taxes, this amount is
    a. a nondeductible item in computing federal taxable income.
    b. a fully deductible item in computing federal taxable income
    c. a deductible item in computing federal taxable income but only to the extent it would not produce a negative taxable income at the federal level.
    d. either a credit or a deduction, at the option of the corporation.
    e. a credit against its federal income tax.

2. When a U.S. corporation incurs a foreign income tax on dividends received from a foreign corporation or from branch operations in a foreign country, this tax is
    a. a nondeductible item in computing U.S. federal taxable income.
    b. a fully deductible item in computing U.S. federal taxable income.
    c. a deductible item in computing U.S. federal taxable income but only to the extent it would not produce a negative taxable income at the federal level
    d. either a credit or a deduction, at the option of the U.S. corporation, in computing its U.S. federal tax liability.
    e. a credit against its U.S. federal income tax.

3. When a corporation incurs state or local property taxes, this amount is
    a. a nondeductible item in computing federal taxable income.
    b. a fully deductible item in computing federal taxable income.
    c. a deductible item in computing federal taxable income but only to the extent it would not produce a negative taxable income at the federal level.
    d. either a credit or a deduction, at the option of the corporation.
    e. a credit against its federal income tax.

Exhibit 2-2 (continued)

4. When a corporation is entitled to take a 7 percent investment tax credit (job development tax credit) due to the purchase of a depreciable asset, the depreciation deduction is
   a. reduced by the amount of the credit in the year the credit is taken.
   b. reduced by the amount of the credit but spread over the tax basis useful life of the asset.
   c. increased by the amount of the credit in the year the credit is taken.
   d. increased by the amount of the credit but spread over the tax basis useful life of the asset.
   e. not affected by the credit.

5. A corporation receives a deduction for both the normal service cost and past service cost of qualified pension plans
   a. as these costs are recorded for book purposes.
   b. as the employee benefits vest.
   c. as the employees receive benefits, but only to the extent these are taxable as ordinary income.
   d. as these costs are funded, except that the past service cost cannot be deducted over a shorter period than 10 years.
   e. as amounts are paid into the fund.

6. When a corporation sells at a gain unimproved land which has been owned and used as a parking area for 18 months, this gain is
   a. taxed as either ordinary gain or long-term capital gain depending on the amounts of other similarly taxed gains or losses.
   b. taxed as short-term capital gain.
   c. taxed as ordinary income.
   d. totally excluded from taxable income.
   e. taxed as long-term capital gain.

7. When a depreciable asset which has been held several years is sold at a gain, the process of depreciation recapture for "excess" depreciation involves
   a. disallowing future depreciation in a like amount on the replacement assets by reducing the basis of the replacement asset.
   b. taxing the smaller of the gain or the excess depreciation as long-term capital gain.
   c. taxing the smaller of the gain or the excess depreciation as short-term capital gain.
   d. taxing the smaller of the gain or the excess depreciation as ordinary income.
   e. taxing the "excess" depreciation as ordinary income.

8. If a corporation in the 48 percent tax bracket has the following investment opportunities, which will produce the highest after tax return on a $1,000,000 investment? (All securities would be sold at the end of one year to yield the rates specified.)
   a. An investment at par in state bonds yielding 8 percent.
   b. An investment at par in bonds of other corporations yielding 16 percent.
   c. An investment in common stock of a nonaffiliated corporation where the yield is 10 percent.
   d. An investment in U.S. Treasury bills yielding 10 percent.
   e. A speculative investment in land which can be sold for $1,124,000 at the end of one year.

9. Percentage depletion for oil and gas production is a fixed percentage (22 percent) of
   a. the gross value (Fair Market Value) of the crude product.
   b. the net value (Fair Market Value less cost of production) of the crude product.
   c. the net value of the refined products.
   d. the gross value of the crude product but not to exceed 50 percent of the taxable income before depletion from this source.
   e. the net value of the crude product but not to exceed 50 percent of the taxable income before depletion from this source.

Exhibit 2-2 (continued)

10. When a consolidated tax return is filed reflecting a consolidated tax liability,
    a. all affiliates included in this consolidted return are jointly and severally liable for the tax.
    b. only the parent company is liable for the tax.
    c. only those affiliates included in this return which would have had positive taxable incomes on a separate return basis are liable for the tax.
    d. only those affiliates included in this return which would have had positive tax liabilities on a separate return basis are liable for the tax.
    e. only a particular designated affiliate is liable for the tax.

11. A Western Hemisphere Trade Corporation (WHTC) is
    a. a foreign corporation taxed in the U.S. to the extent it does business in the Western Hemisphere.
    b. a domestic corporation which receives a special tax deduction for doing business primarily in the Western Hemisphere but outside the U.S.
    c. a domestic corporation doing business primarily in the Western Hemisphere and tax exempt on business done outside of the U.S.
    d. a corportion located outside the U.S. but within the Western Hemisphere and is tax exempt on business done in the U.S.
    e. another name for a domestic international sales corporation.

12. As interest rates rise the market values of outstanding bonds tend to fall; thus a company may acquire outstanding bonds and retire them at a gain. This gain is
    a. either taxed as ordinary income or deferred over a period not to exceed 10 years.
    b. taxed as long-term capital gain.
    c. either taxed as ordinary income or deferred by reducing the basis of specific assets.
    d. recognized as ordinary income proportionately over the remaining life of the old issue.
    e. Excluded from taxation.

13. A corporation has $200,000 of taxable net operating income, $20,000 of interest income from taxable sources and $10,000 of dividends from investment in other domestic corporations and $30,000 of net long-term capital gains in excess of short-term capital losses. What is the maximum cash contribution it can make to a university and currently deduct it?
    a. $13,000   d. $12,575
    b. $11,500   e. $12,250
    c. $10,000

14. Under the asset depreciation range class life system (often referred to as ADR) if an asset has a guideline life of 15 years its useful life for depreciation purposes would be
    a. 13.5 years.
    b. 12 years.
    c. any life from 12 to 18 years.
    d. any life from 13.5 years to 16.5 years.
    e. some length of time other than those listed above.

15. When can a French corporation doing business in the U.S. be included in a consolidated tax return of an affiliated group of domestic corporations?
    a. When one member of the existing group acquires at least 70 percent of the voting stock of that foreign corporation.
    b. When the parent corporation acquires at least 80 percent of the voting stock of that foreign corporation.
    c. When the affiliated group as a whole acquires at least 80 percent of the voting stock of that foreign corporation

Exhibit 2-2 (continued)
- d. When the affiliated group as a whole acquires at least 51 percent of the voting stock of that foreign corporation.
- e. Such foreign corporations cannot be included in a U.S. tax return even if they are owned 100 percent by the U.S. parent.

16. Which of the following is **not** a purpose of the Securities Exchange Act of 1934?
    - a. to establish federal regulation over securities exchanges and markets.
    - b. to prevent unfair practices on securities exchanges and markets.
    - c. to discourage and prevent the use of credit in financing excessive speculation in securities.
    - d. to approve the securities of corporations which are to be traded publicly.
    - e. to control unfair use of information by corporate insiders.

17. The form and content for financial statements filed with the Securities and Exchange Commission (SEC) are specified in
    - a. SEC accounting series releases.
    - b. SEC regulation S-X.
    - c. the statements of the Financial Accounting Standards Board.
    - d. the Securities Acts of 1933 and 1934.
    - e. the Securities Acts Amendments of 1964.

18. The Securities and Exchange Commission (SEC) defines a material line of business as one which provides
    - a. 15 percent or more of the company's total sales and revenues provided revenue exceeded $50,000,000 in both of the last two fiscal years.
    - b. 10 percent or more of the income (before income tax and extraordinary items) computed with deduction of loss resulting from any line of business provided revenues exceeded $50,000,000 in either of the last two fiscal years.
    - c. 15 percent or more of the income (before income tax and extraordinary items) computed without deduction of loss resulting from any line of business provided revenues exceeded $50,000,000 in both of the last two fiscal years.
    - d. 10 percent or more of the company's total sales and revenues provided revenue is over $50,000,000 in either of the last two fiscal years.
    - e. 10 percent or more of the company's total sales and revenues provided revenue is less than $50,000,000 in either of the last two fiscal years.

19. The Financial Accounting Standards Board (FASB) was proposed by
    - a. the American Institute of Certified Public Accountants
    - b. the Accounting Principles Board.
    - c. the Study Group on the Objectives of Financial Statements (Trueblood Committee).
    - d. the Securities and Exchange Commission.
    - e. a Special Study Group on Establishment of Accounting Principles (Wheat Committee).

20. The Financial Accounting Foundation is governed by a nine-member Board of Trustees. Which of the following is **not** one of the primary duties of the Board of Trustees?
    - a. to arrange for the financing of the organization.
    - b. to appoint the members of the Financial Accounting Advisory Council.
    - c. to prepare and administer the budget of the Financial Accounting Foundation.
    - d. to appoint the members of the Financial Accounting Standards Board.
    - e. to work closely with the FASB in an advisory capacity in development of accounting standards.

21. The major distinction between the Financial Accounting Standards Board (FASB) and its predecessor, the Accounting Principles Board (APB), is
    - a. the FASB issues exposure drafts of proposed standards.

Exhibit 2-2 (continued)

    b. all members of the FASB are fully remunerated, serve full time, and are independent of any companies or institutions.
    c. all members of the FASB possess extensive experience in financial reporting.
    d. a majority of the members of the FASB are CPAs drawn from public practice.
    e. interpretations by the FASB will be issued when necessary.

22. The Cost Accounting Standards Board (CASB) was established by
    a. the Accounting Principles Board (APB)
    b. **the Governmental Accounting Office (GAO)**
    c. the Financial Accounting Standards Board (FASB)
    d. the U.S. Congress.
    e. the Securities and Exchange Commission (SEC).

23. The Cost Accounting Standards Board's (CASB) purpose is to
    a. develop accounting principles and standard practices for industry.
    b. develop uniform cost accounting standards to be used in pricing, administration and settlement of negotiated defense contracts and subcontracts with relevant federal agencies.
    c. work in conjunction with the Securities and Exchange Commission (SEC) in examining registration forms and statements filed by corporations.
    d. administer all contracts and subcontracts with federal agencies.
    e. aid the Financial Accounting Standards Board (FASB) in establishing accounting standards.

24. The cost standards issued by the Cost Accounting Standards Board (CASB)
    a. are ratified directly by vote of both houses of Congress.
    b. require consensus from industry to make the standard legal.
    c. become law after 60 days from the date of publication in the Federal Register for the second time provided Congress does not enact a resolution in opposition.
    d. become law once they are approved by the CASB.
    e. are suggested guidelines which companies are asked to adopt and follow.

25. The disclosure concept as used in financial reporting requires that
    a. all information relevant to users be reported in the president's letter to the stockholders.
    b. all information relevant to users be reported in the body of the financial statements.
    c. all information relevant to users be reported in the footnotes to the financial statements.
    d. all information relevent to users be reported in the body of or footnotes to the financial statements.
    e. all information relevant to users be reported in the company's discussion of products and product lines, operating results, and future plans and commitments.

26. The consistency concept as used in accounting requires that
    a. related revenues and expenses be recognized in the same accounting period.
    b. like transactions be treated in the same manner in different periods.
    c. a business entity must continue to use the same reporting or valuation methods once a method has been adopted.
    d. a business entity report events in a manner which minimizes current income.
    e. a business entity use the same independent auditor each year.

27. When price-level adjusted statements are presented in the United States according to Accounting Principles Board Statement No. 3, Financial Statements Restated for General-Price-Level Changes, assets are

Exhibit 2-2 (continued)

    a. valued at current cost.
    b. **valued at replacement cost.**
    c. valued at net realizable value.
    d. valued at the current general purchasing power equivalent of historical cost.
    e. valued at an alternative amount not enumerated above.

28. Goodwill should be written off
    a. as soon as possible against retained earnings.
    b. as soon as possible against the investment account.
    c. by systematic charges to retained earnings over the period benefited, but not more than 40 years.
    d. by systematic charges to expense over the period benefited, but not more than 40 years.
    e. by some other method that is not described above.

29. The unamortized discount on bonds payable
    a. should be shown as an asset on the balance sheet.
    b. should be expensed immediately.
    c. should be shown as a liability on the balance sheet.
    d. should be shown on the balance sheet as a deduction from the maturity value of the bonds.
    e. should be reported as a loss on issuance of bonds.

30. Bond issue costs
    a. should be charged as an expense when incurred.
    b. should be charged **against retained earnings when incurred.**
    c. should be amortized over the life of the bonds to which they apply.
    d. should be included in organization costs.
    e. should be charged to interest expense when incurred.

31. The market value of marketable securities.
    a. is required to be disclosed in balance sheet presentations.
    b. is required to be disclosed only if it is less than cost.
    c. is required to be disclosed if significantly different from cost.
    d. is not required to be disclosed.
    e. may or may not be disclosed at the discretion of management.

32. Contingent liabilities
    a. should be disclosed in footnotes to the financial statements if material.
    b. should be shown as current liabilities in the balance sheet.
    c. should be shown as long-term liabilities in the balance sheet.
    d. are valued at their net present values.
    e. need not be disclosed because few of them ever materialize into real liabilities.

The following Data Applies to Items 33-37

The Asan Corporation manufactures industrial equipment in the United States. It owns 75 percent of the stock of Asan Corporation of Canada, 80 percent of the stock of Asan Corporation of Africa and 100 percent of the stock of Asan Credit Corpoartion. Asan Corporation prepares consolidated financial statements consolidating Asan of Canada and uses the equity method for Asan of Africa and Asan Credit. Data from the reports of these companies are shown below.

Exhibit 2-2 (continued)

	1973 Net Income	1973 Dividends Paid
Asan Corp.- Consolidated	$1,400,000	$250,000
Asan of Canada	120,000	100,000
Asan of Africa	70,000	40,000
Asan Credit	90,000	60,000

33. How much of the net income reported by Asan Corporation Consolidated is attributable to the operations of the three subsidiaries?
   a. $280,000
   b. $200,000.
   c. $236,000.
   d. $167,000.
   e. $266,000.

34. If all three subsidiaries had been consolidated the net income reported by Asan Corporation Consolidated would be
   a. $1,400,000.
   b. $1,359,000.
   c. $1,411,000.
   d. $1,164,000.
   e. some amount other than those enumerated above.

35. The minority interest in Asan Corporation Consolidated is credited with the following amount of income for 1973:
   a. $190,000.
   b. $140,000.
   c. $33,000.
   d. $44,000.
   e. $30,000.

36. Which of the following changes would **not** affect the reported net income of Asan Corporation Consolidated?
   a. if Asan of Canada's income were $150,000 rather than $120,000.
   b. if Asan of Africa's income were $50,000 rather than $70,000.
   c. if Asan Credit dividends were $70,000 rather than $60,000.
   d. if Asan Credit's income were $100,000 rather than $90,000.
   e. if Asan Consolidated dividends were $275,000 rather than $250,000.

37. There have been internal disorders in the country where Asan of Africa is located. It has been suggested that the consolidation policy of Asan Corporation be revised with respect to Asan of Africa to follow the cost method of accounting for investments.
   a. This method would not change the reported income of Asan Corporation Consolidated.
   b. The reported income of Asan Corporation Consolidated would decline by $30,000.
   c. The reported income of Asan Corporation Consolidated would decline by $24,000.
   d. The cost method is not an acceptable method of accounting for a subsidiary in any circumstances.
   e. None of the above answers is appropriate.

Exhibit 2-2 (continued)

PART 4

QUESTION NUMBER 4—Estimated time 3/4 hour

The **Metropolitan News**, a daily newspaper, services a community of 100,000. The paper has a cirulation of 40,000, with 32,000 copies delivered directly to subscribers. The rate schedule for the paper is:

	Daily	Sunday
Single issue price	$0.15	$0.30
Weekly subscription		$1.00
(Includes daily and Sunday)		

The paper has experienced profitable operations as can be seen from the Income Statement for the Year Ended September 30, 1974 (000 omitted):

Revenue		
Newspaper Sales	$2,200	
Advertising Sales	1,800	$4,000
Costs and Expenses		
Personnel Costs		
Commissions		
Carriers	$ 292	
Sales	73	
Advertising	48	
Salaries		
Administration	250	
Advertising	100	
Equipment Operators	500	
Newsroom	400	
Employee Benefits	195	$1,858
Newsprint		834
Other Supplies		417
Repairs		25
Depreciation		180
Property Taxes		120
Building Rental		80
Automobile Leases		10
Other		90
Total Costs and Expenses		$3,614
Income Before Income Taxes		$ 386
Income Taxes		154
Net Income		$ 232

Exhibit 2-2 (continued)

The Sunday edition usually has twice as many pages as the daily editions. Analysis of direct edition variable costs for 1973-74 is shown in the schedule below.

	Cost per Issue	
	Daily	Sunday
Paper	$0.050	$0.100
Other Supplies	0.025	0.050
Carrier and Sales Commission	0.025	0.025
	$0.100	$0.175

Several changes in operations are scheduled for the next year, in addition to the need to recognize increasing costs.

1. The building lease expired on September 30, 1974 and has been renewed with a change in the rental fee provisions from a straight fee to a fixed fee of $60,000 plus 1 percent of newspaper sales.

2. The advertising department will eliminate the payment of a 4 percent advertising commission on contracts sold by its employees. An average of two-thirds of the advertising has been sold on a contract basis in the past. The salaries of the four who solicited advertising will be raised from $7,500 each to $14,000 each.

3. Automobiles will no longer be leased. Employees whose jobs require automobiles will use their own and be reimbursed at $0.15 per mile. The leased cars were driven 80,000 miles in 1973-74, and it is estimated that the employees will drive some 84,000 miles next year on company business.

4. Cost increases estimated for next year:
  a. Newsprint $0.01 per daily issue and $0.02 for the Sunday paper
  b. Salaries:
    (1) Equipment operators   8%
    (2) Other employees   6%
  c. Employee benefits (From 15% of   5%
     personnel costs excluding carrier and
     sales commissions to 20%)

5. Circulation increases of 5 percent in newsstand and home delivery are anticipated.

6. Advertising revenue is estimated at $1,890,000 with $1,260,000 from employee solicited contracts.

Required:

A. Prepare a projected income statement for the **Metropolitan News** for the 1974-75 fiscal year using a format which shows the total variable costs and total fixed costs for the newspaper (round calculations to the nearest thousand dollars).

B. The management of **Metropolitan News** is contemplating one aditional proposal for the 1974-75 fiscal year raising the rates for its newspaper to the following amounts:

	Daily	Sunday
Single issue price	$0.20	$0.40
Weekly subscription (includes daily and Sunday)		$1.25

Exhibit 2-2 (continued)

It is estimated that the newspaper's circulation would decline to 90 percent of the currently anticipated 1974-75 level for both newsstand and home delivery sales if this change is initiated. Calculate the effect on the projected 1974-75 income if this proposed rate change is implemented.

PART 5

QUESTION NUMBER 2—Estimated time ½ hour

The Ramon Co. manufactures a wide range of products at several different plant locations. The Franklin Plant, which manufactures electrical components, has been experiencing some difficulties with fluctuating monthly overhead costs. The fluctuations have made it difficult to estimate the level of overhead that will be incurred for any one month.

Management wants to be able to estimate overhead costs accurately in order to plan its operation and financial needs better. A trade association publication to which Ramon Co. subscribes indicates that, for companies manufacturing electrical components, overhead tends to vary with direct labor hours.

One member of the accounting staff has proposed that the cost behavior pattern of the overhead costs be determined. Then overhead costs could be predicted from the budgeted direct labor hours.

Another member of the accounting staff suggested that a good starting place for determining the cost behavior pattern of overhead costs would be an analysis of historical data. The historical cost behavior pattern would provide a basis for estimating future overhead costs. The methods proposed for determining the cost behavior pattern included the high-low method, the scattergraph method, simple linear regression, multiple regression, and exponential smoothing. Of these methods Ramon Co. decided to employ the high-low method, the scattergraph method, and simple linear regression. Data on direct labor hours and the respective overhead costs incurred were collected for the past two years. The raw data and the scattergraph prepared from the data are as follows:

1973	Direct Labor Hours	Overhead Costs
January	20,000	$84,000
February	25,000	99,000
March	22,000	89,500
April	23,000	90,000
May	20,000	81,500
June	19,000	75,500
July	14,000	70,500
August	10,000	64,500
September	12,000	69,000
October	17,000	75,000
November	16,000	71,500
December	19,000	78,000

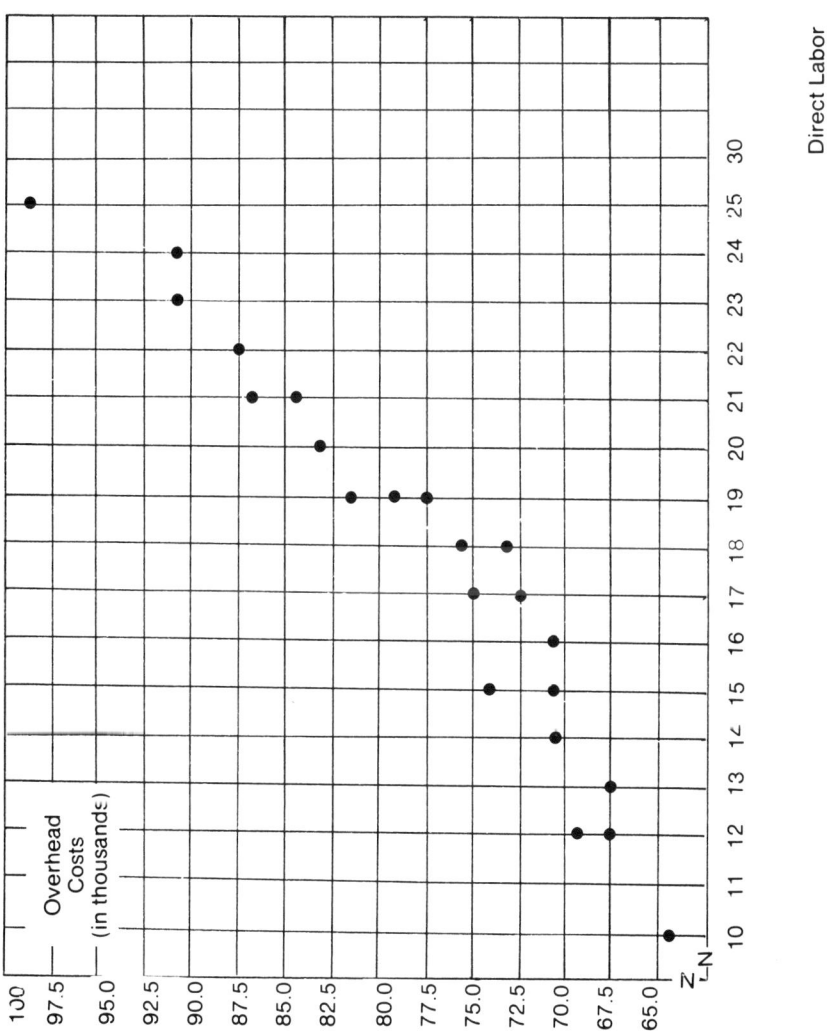

Exhibit 2-2 (continued)

Exhibit 2-2 (continued)

1974

January	21,000	86,000
February	24,000	93,000
March	23,000	93,000
April	22,000	87,000
May	20,000	80,000
June	18,000	76,500
July	12,000	67,500
August	13,000	71,000
September	15,000	73,500
October	17,000	72,500
November	15,000	71,000
December	18,000	75,000

Using linear regression, the following data were obtained:

Coefficient of determination	.9109
Coefficient of correlation	.9544
Coefficients of regression equation	
Constant	39,859
Independent variable	2.1549
Standard error of the estimate	2,840
Standard error of the regression	
Coefficient for the independent variable	.1437
True t-statistic for a 95% confidence interval	
(22 degrees of freedom)	2.074

Required:

A. Using the high-low method, determine the cost behavior pattern of the overhead costs for the Franklin Plant.

B. Using the results of the regression analysis, calculate the estimate of overhead costs for 22,500 direct labor hours.

C. Of the three proposed methods (high-low, scattergraph, linear regression), which one should Ramon Co. employ to determine the historical cost behavior pattern of Franklin Plant's overhead costs? Explain your answer completely, indicating the reasons why the other methods should not be used.

222 Unofficial Solutions

Exhibit 2-3 shows the unofficial solutions to the CMA exam questions in the preceding section.

Exhibit 2-3
Unofficial Solutions
PART 1

QUESTION NUMBER 6

A. The cost of capital for a firm is computed as a weighted average of the component costs of the sources utilized to raise capital where the weights relate to the percentage of total capital raised. In this case, the two components are debt and equity.

Exhibit 2-3 (continued)

$$\text{Cost of debt } (K_i) = (\text{interest rate}) \times (1\text{-tax rate})$$
$$\text{Cost of equity } (K_e) = \left(\frac{\text{dividend}}{\text{price}}\right) + \text{growth}$$
$$\text{Cost of capital } (K_o) = (\text{weight of debt}) \times (K_i) + (\text{weight of equity}) \times (K_e)$$

Alternative A
$$K_i = .09(1 - .5) = 4.5\%$$
$$K_e = \frac{\$1 + .07}{\$20} = 12\%$$
$$K_o = \left(\frac{2}{6}\right) \times (.045) + \left(\frac{4}{6}\right) \times (.12) = 9.5\%$$

Alternative B
$$K_i = .12(1 - .5) = 6\%$$
$$K_e = \frac{\$.90 + .12}{\$20} = 16.5\%$$
$$K_o = \left(\frac{4}{6}\right) \times (.06) + \left(\frac{2}{6}\right) \times (.165) = 9.5\%$$

The weighted average cost of capital is the same for Alternatives A and B because the risk-return trade offs for A and B balance each other.

B The interest rate on debt is higher for Alternative B because the financial risk is greater due to the increased use of leverage. As a result, the probability of not being able to meet the high fixed payment increases, causing the bond market to offset this greater risk with a higher required rate of return.

C. It is logical for shareholders to expect a higher dividend growth rate under Alternative B because of the additional financial risk and increased fixed interest requirement. Equity holders will demand a higher return to compensate them for the additional financial risk. Also dividends per share should grow at a faster rate because earnings per share grow faster due to the greater amount of leverage (smaller base) and, assuming a given payout rate, it follows that dividends per share would also grow faster.

Note: Material from the Certificate in Management Accounting Examinations, Copyright © 1074 by the National Association of Accountants, is reprinted with permission.

PART 2

QUESTION NUMBER 5

A.
  1. The treasurer is primarily concerned with short-run profit maximization.
  2. The sales vice president expreses two goals——maximization of sales volume and market share.
  3. The production vice president is concerned about producing a high quality product and promoting productivity and operating efficiency.
  4. The president should be concerned with the overall activities of the firm. However, he appears to be primarily concerned with the company image. In addition, he appears to be interested in maintaining good labor relations.

72   The Bottom Line

Exhibit 2-3 (continued)

B. In classical theory, the goal of the firm is profit maximization. To some degree the objectives of the treasurer are compatible with classical economic theory. However, modern economists recognize the necessity of balancing both long-range and short-range profitability with risk in setting optimum profit goals.

Each of the individual executives cited in this case have failed to recognize the need to balance their technically oriented sub-goals with the broader economic goals of the total organization.

PART 3

QUESTION NUMBER 1

1. b	10. a	19. e	28. d
2. d	11. b	20. e	29. d
3. b	12. c	21. b	30. c
4. e	13. a	22. d	31. d, e
5. d	14. c	23. b	32. a
6. a	15. e	24. c	33. c
7. d	16. d	25. d	34. a
8. c	16. b	26. b	35. e
9. d	18. d	27. d	36. c, e
			37. d

PART 4

QUESTION NUMBER 4

A.

Metropolitan News
Projected Income Statement
For the Year Ended September 30, 1975
(000 omitted)

Revenue:			
Newspaper sales (2,200 × 1.05)			$2,310
Advertising sales			1,890
Total revenue			$4,200
Variable costs:			
Commissions:			
Carriers (292 × 1.05)	$307		
Sales (73 × 1.05)	77	$ 384	
Newsprint (834 × 1.2 × 1.05)		1,051	
Other supplies (417 × 1.05)		438	
Building rental (2,310 × .01)		23	
Total variable costs			1,896
Contribution margin			$2,304
Fixed costs:			
Salaries:			
Administration (250 × 1.06)	$265		
Advertising [(4 × 14) + [100 −			
(4 × 7.5)] × 1.06]	130		
Equipment operators (500 × 1.08)	540		

Exhibit 2-3 (continued)

Newsroom (400 × 1.06)	424	
Employee benefits (1,359 × .2)	272	$1,631
Repairs		25
Depreciation		180
Property taxes		120
Building rental		60
Automobile expenses (84,000 × .15)		13
Other		90
Total fixed costs		2,119
Net income before income taxes		$ 185
Net taxes (40%)		74
Net income		$ 111

B. Change in revenue (000 omitted)
Revenue under proposed structure:

Weekly subscriptions (2,310 × .8 × .9 × 1.25)		$2,079
Newsstand sales (2,310 × .2 × .9 × 1.333)		554
Total revenue under proposed structure		$2,633
Revenue under present price structure:		2,310
Increased revenue		$ 323

Changes in costs:

Building rental (323 × .01)	$ 3	
Carrier commissions (307 × .10)	(31)	
Sales commissions (77 × .10)	(8)	
Newsprint (1,051 × .10)	(105)	
Other supplies (438 × .10)	(44)	
Net decreases in costs		$ (185)
Increase in net income before income taxes		$ 508
Income taxes (40%)		203
Increase in net income		$ 305

PART 5

QUESTION NUMBER 2

A.

	Direct Labor Hours (DLH)	Overhead Costs
High (February 1973)	25,000	$99,000
Low (August 1973)	10,000	64,500
Difference	15,000	$34,500

Slope of line (variable cost rate) = $\frac{\$34,500}{15,000 \text{ DLH}}$

= $2.30 per DLH

Total overhead costs at 25,000 DLH	$99,000
Variable overhead costs (25,000 × $2.30)	57,500
Fixed overhead	$41,500

Exhibit 2-3 (continued)

Total overhead cost = Fixed overhead cost +
 (Variable cost rate per DLH ×
 Direct labor hours)

= $41,500 + $2.30X, where X =
 number of DLH

B. Total overhead cost
 = Fixed overhead cost + Variable cost rate per
  DLH × DLH
 = $39,859 + $2.1549X (where X = DLH)
 = $39,859 + $2.1549 (22,500)
 = $39,859 + $48,485.25
 = $88,344.25

C. The data seem to indicate that the regression line of Y = 39,859 + 2.1549X, where X = DLH, provides a good estimate of the cost behavior of overhead costs. The coefficient of determination indicates that over 90 percent of the total variation in total overhead costs can be explained by the regression equation. The standard error of the estimate ($2,840) is reasonable for the level of costs involved. The standard error of the regression coefficient for the independent variable (direct labor hours) is small relative to the coefficient. These observations seem to indicate that the regression analysis might be adequate for determining the historical cost behavior pattern of overhead costs.

A visual examination of the data presented in the graph suggests that there is either a curvilinear relationship or a change in the cost behavior pattern between 19,000 and 20,000 direct labor hours. For this reason, it might be appropriate for Ramon Co. to use the scattergraph approach and derive a curvilinear relationship or a relationship represented by two line segments. If a single straight line were to be drawn, the linear regression method would probably provide a better estimate of the relationship because it is difficult to represent all the information properly with a line drawn subjectively.

A combination of scattergraph analysis and linear regression may be more appropriate in this case. The scattergraph would help identify extreme data points that should be ignored and would suggest two linear regressions, one on each side of 19,000-20,000 DLH.

Ramon Co. should not employ the high-low method because this method employs only two pieces of the raw data and discards the rest. This method uses (by definition) the two extreme points which in this case appear to be abnormal.

223 How to Prepare to Take the CMA Exam

The CMA examination is a test covering, for the most part, material included in undergraduate and graduate accounting curricula. The accounting graduate with a good standing in college may be able to pass the examination. Additional concentrated study in individual weak areas would improve the chances for successfully completing the exam. The CMA exam places more emphasis on economics and business finance, the use and application of quantitative methods, and in management accounting than does the CPA exam. However, there is less emphasis placed on accounting pronouncements by the accounting regulatory bodies.

The American Accounting Association's Committee on Professional Examinations studied the material covered in the CPA, CMA, and CIA (Certified Internal Auditor) examinations during the year 1974-75. They observed that "The CMA examination requires a broader understanding of many topics in accounting, finance, and general business subjects than does the CPA or CIA examination. The CPA examination requires consistently high levels of competency in accounting topics but does not require intensive preparation for nonaccounting topics such as quantitative methods and basic behavioral topics."[1]

230 SPECIAL ENROLLMENT EXAM TO PRACTICE BEFORE IRS

Permission to practice before the IRS is restricted to attorneys, CPAs and those individuals who are technically competent in tax matters. An applicant who does not qualify for either of the first two categories must demonstrate his competence by receiving a passing grade on the Special Enrollment exam (unless he is a former Service employee who meets the requirements of section 10.4, Circular 230).

The examination is administered annually in September in cities containing Internal Revenue district headquarters offices. In the past it has also been available in additional cities when a sufficient number of applicants requested the additional test sites.

The exam consists of three parts (three hours each) administered over a day-and-a-half period. Subjects covered include federal taxes and tax accounting for individuals, partnerships, corporations, trusts and estates, and conference and practice requirements under provisions of Treasury Department Circular 230. The minimum passing score varies from year to year because it is based on a grading curve with a passing rate of approximately 60 percent of the total number of candidates sitting for the exam that year.

231 Sample Examinations

The IRS has published a sample enrollment examination (Department of the Treasury Publication 693). This sample examination provides information concerning the subject coverage and the general format of the exam. This booklet can be obtained from any local IRS office. Past examinations and solutions may be obtained from Commerce Clearing House and Prentice-Hall, Inc. Sample questions from the examination are shown in Exhibit 2-4.

Exhibit 2-4
The following statements are either True or False. Indicate your selection by filling the appropriate space provided on the answer sheet. Where True, fill in "A" where False, fill in "B."

1. A divorced parent having custody who remarries is now allowed to consider support provided by the new spouse in determining who contributed over half the support of the children from the previous marriage.

---

1. "Report of the Committee on Professional Examinations," *Accounting Review*, supplement to vol. XLXI (1976), p. 28.

Exhibit 2-4 (continued)

2. You must file an income tax return if you had net earnings from self employment of $400 or more.
3. On a joint return, only one taxpayer can be considered as being self employed.
4. If you own more than one business, you may not use a different method of accounting for each separate business.
5. If you are an individual who may be claimed as the dependent of another taxpayer and you have unearned income, you must file a return when your gross income is $750 or more.
6. If you are an individual taxpayer and use a fiscal year, you income tax return is due on or before the 15th day of the 3rd month after the close of your tax year.
7. An executor, administrator or legal representative of a calendar year taxpayer who died during the year, must file the decedent's final income tax return, if one is required, by April 15 of the following year.
8. If a farmer or a fisherman with net tax liability of over $100 does not file his income tax return for 1973 by February 1, 1974 he is required to file a declaration of estimated tax.
9. Employees receiving cash tips (one employer) during March 1974 of $20 or more must report them to their employer by April 10, 1974.
10. A calendar year corporation that meets certain requirements and who wishes not to be taxed as a corporation for 1974 must make a subchapter "S" election by February 15, 1974.
11. A corporation will receive a three month extension for filing Form 1120 by filing an application for extension on or before the due date and paying 50% of the remaining tax due.
12. A calendar year partnership must file Form 1065 for 1973 on or before March 15. 1974.
13. An Employer's Federal Tax Return (Form 941) with a balance due must be filed on or before th last day of the month following the end of a calendar quarter.
14. If, at the end of the first month of a quarter, the cumulative amount of undeposited employment taxes is $200.00 or more and less than $2,000 you must deposit the taxes on or before the last day of the following month.
15. An employee may exempt himself from social security taxes (F.I.C.A.) by filing form W4E with his employer.

Note: Reprinted from Department of the Treasury, *Special Enrollment Exam,* Publication 693 (Washington, D.C.: Government Printing Office, rev. June 1975), p.3.

232 How to Prepare to Take the Special Enrollment Examination to Practice before the IRS

The candidate should request a sample booklet containing a special enrollment examination from the local IRS office. This booklet contains typical questions concerning the topics tested in the three parts of the examination. The candidate should refer to section 375 of this publication for guidance in selecting reference material covering the matters. In addition, the candidate may also obtain past examinations and solutions from Commerce Clearing House and Prentice-Hall. These questions and solutions provide excellent material for review and study and will be helpful in identifying those areas most commonly selected for testing.

Persons interested in taking the Special Enrollment exam to practice before the Internal Revenue Service should contact their local IRS office and obtain Treasury Department Circular No. 230 and an application form for the Special Enrollment exam.

240 CHARTERED FINANCIAL ANALYSTS EXAMINATION

The main objective of the C.F.A. examinations is to assure the investing public, employers, and fellow analysts that the candidate possesses the fundamental knowledge necessry to practice the profession. The C.F.A. designation was established to provide a means of rating and applying a professional title to those people involved in investment research and portfolio management or supervision of investment funds. Financial analysts are also in all segments of the financial industry, including commercial banking, brokerage and investment banking, insurance, investment counseling, mutual funds, endorsement and pension or profit-sharing funds, and financial publishing.

The C.F.A. exams are administered yearly by the Institute of Chartered Financial Analysts in centers located throughout the United States and in several foreign countries. The examinations are part of an overall C.F.A. program established to recognize proficiency in the area of financial analysis and to further develop and encourage a high level of ethical standards for the professional analyst.

Material in this section was adapted from *The C.F.A. Announcement, 1977-1978* (Charlottesville, Va.: The Institute of Chartered Financial Analysts, 1977).

241 The C.F.A. Candidate Study Program

THE C.F.A. CANDIDATE STUDY PROGRAM

The specific contents of the C.F.A. study materials and examinations are subject to modifications in order to keep pace with changing emphasis and techniques in financial analysis.

The specific contents of the C.F.A. study materials and examinations are subject to modifications in order to keep pace with changing emphasis and techniques in financial analysis.

Candidates who have been approved for a particular study program and who have paid the applicable enrollment fee will receive a Study Guide containing a detailed reading list prepared specifically for C.F.A. candidates. There is no additional charge to such candidates for this material. A limited number of copies is available for purchase by non-candidates.

While the Institute itself does not offer classroom-type courses of instruction, it does assist in the organization of local study groups in conjunction with the C.F.A. Educational Coordinators of local analyst societies and universities. Of special assistance to candidates are the Study Guides, textbooks, and books of readings published periodically by the Institute.

The C.F.A. is awarded to those candidates who have successfully completed the examinations and other requirements established by The Institute of Chartered Financial Analysts. The candidate must, in sequential order, pass three examinations: The C.F.A. Preliminary Examination (C.F.A. I); Examination II—Applied Financial Analysis; and Examination III—Investment Management.

The main objective of the C.F.A. Candidate Study Program and Examination Series is to assure the investing public, employers, and fellow analysts that a C.F.A possesses at least the fundamental knowledge necessary to practice his profession. There are seven basic topic areas extending through the study series: Economics, Financial Accounting, Quantitative Techniques, Fixed Income Securities Analysis, Equity Securities Analysis, Portfolio Management, and Professional Standards. The C.F.A. study program necessarily continues to be of an evolutionary nature, reflecting as it does the changing emphasis and techniques of financial analysis and portfolio management in the dynamic economies of the United States and Canada. The logic and objectives of the program may best be illustrated by the following brief review of the seven main subject areas. More specific study guidance to candidates is provided in each of the three Study Guides published annually by the institute.[2]

242 The C.F.A. Competency Standards

The C.F.A. Competency Standards

Although the subject matter and skills needed by a C.F.A. continue to evolve, the principal areas and topics to be mastered by C.F.A. candidates are suggested by the topic areas described   below and listed in the *General Topic Outline*. The examinee level I study program is designed for the junior analyst, while the program at levels II and III is intended for analysts at progressively more advanced stages of professional development. Consequently, the candidate study program emphasizes the continuity of required subject matter over the three different levels as well as a progression to higher levels of sophistication involving more complex financial problems. In addition, at the progressively more advanced levels, the experienced candidate is expected to deal with an expanded number of topics.[3]

---

2. Reprinted from *The C.F.A. Announcement, 1977-78* (Charlottesville, Va.: The Institute of Charted Financial Analysts, 1977), p. 6.
3. Ibid., p. 7.

243 The C.F.A. Examination

AREA ONE—ECONOMICS
Pre-Candidate Requirements

The examinee should be familiar with the basic principles of macroeconomics and the monetary system. The analyst should have a minimum knowledge equivalent to one academic year of principles of economics as reflected in an elementary economics textbook. C.F.A. examinations, however, emphasize the practical application of economic concepts rather than abstract economic and monetary theories.

C.F.A. Prelfiminary Examination (C.F.A. Level I)

The examinee should be familiar with the tools of economic analysis and forecasting and have a perspective of the history of economic and industrial activity and of the structure of money and capital markets. Primary emphasis is placed on the relevance and application of economics to the analysis of investment securities.

C.F.A. Level II

The candidate should be able to apply basic economic concepts and techniques, studied under C.F.A. Level I, to an evaluation of specific industries and companies. Emphasis is placed on forecasting broad economic forces and their implications for projections of interest rates, aggregate corporate earnings, and the level of security prices.

C.F.A. Level III

The candidate should be able to interpret economic conditions, government policies and actions, and their effects on the growth of the economy, inflation, and employment. The analyst is expected to understand the implications of these policies and conditions and to relate these to a penetrating analysis of aggregate corporate earnings, of earnings trends in specific industries and companies, of interest rates, and of security prices. This analysis should be used to formulate investment policy decisions.

AREA TWO—FINANCIAL ACCOUNTING
Pre-Candidate Requirements

The examinee should understand the principles of accounting equivalent to at least one academic year of accounting.

C.F.A. Preliminary Examination (C.F.A. Level I)

The examinee should be able to apply accounting principles and techniques to financial analysis. Emphasis is placed on skill in using published accounting data, including corporate financial statements and reports, in a meaningful analysis of companies.

C.F.A Level II

The candidate should have a sufficiently thorough understanding of financial accounting—including such areas as mergers and acquisitions, inventory and plant valuation, foreign exchange gains and losses, pension plans and leases—to interpret financial statements for use in the proper evaluation of companies and securities. Candidates are expected to be familiar with the opinion and decisions of the Financial Accounting Standards Board, as well as the opinions and decisions of regulatory authorities and the former Accounting Principles Board.

C.F.A. Level III

In addition to the knowledge required at Levels I and II, the candidate is expected to be able to relate accounting data to the investment decision-making process with emphasis on portfolio management.

AREA THREE—QUANTITATIVE TECHNIQUES

Pre-Candidate Requirements

The examinee should have some familiarity with elementry statistics and basic mathematics.

C.F.A. Preliminary Examination (C.F.A. Level I)

The examinee should have a sufficient understanding of elementary statistics and mathematics of finance to be able to work with statistical data and to apply a knowledge of statistical techniques to basic problems in finance and financial analysis.

C.F.A Level II

In addition to the knowledge of Level I, a candidate is expected to be familiar with more advanced techniques—such as probability theory, hypothesis testing, and simple and multiple regression and correlation analysis—and to be able to apply these techniques to problems of financial projections, portfolio analysis, and security valuation and risk.

C.F.A Level III

At this further advanced level, the candidate is expected to understand the application of more sophisticated statistical techniques and systems to problems in financial analysis, capital markets, and portfolio selection.

AREA FOUR—FIXED-INCOME SECURITIES ANALYSIS

Pre-Candidate Requirements

The examinee should have the equivalent of two years of college study in business administration—including business finance, corporate financial analysis, and money and banking (or money and capital markets).

C.F.A Preliminary Examination (C.F.A. Level I)

The examinee is expected to be able to analyze and understand the basic features and characteristics of fixed-income securities—corporate bonds, national and local government bonds, straight preferred stocks, and convertable debentures and preferreds. The analyst should be able to determine the basic investment quality and value of fixed-income securities in terms of yield and the risk of corporate illiquidity or even insolvency. The examinee should understand the basic nature and cause of bond price fluctuations and the exposure of fixed-income securities to interest rate risk and purchasing power risk.

C.F.A. Level II

At this level, the candidate should have an understanding of the financial and investment implications of the elements and characteristics of fixed-income securities. The analyst should be able to analyze, in some depth, government and corporate issuers and their fixed-income securities. The candidate should understand the implications of the interest rate structure, yield spreads, and yield curve.

C.F.A. Level III

In addition to the knowledge required at Levels I and II, the candidate should be able to analyze bond swaps and problems of marketability. Emphasis at this level is placed on the management of fixed-income securities in a portfolio situation and their suitability to both objectives and contraints of different investors under changing economic and market conditions.

AREA FIVE—EQUITY SECURITIES ANALYSIS

Pre-Candidate Requirements

The examinee is assumed to have the equivalent of two years of college study in business administration—including business finance, corporate financial analysis, and either money and banking or money and capital markets.

C.F.A Preliminary Examination (C.F.A Level I)

The examinee should be able to appraise industries and companies from a financial and investment point of view. The analyst should understand and interpret ordinary types of financial data and thereby demonstrate an ability to appraise the value and risks of common stocks.

C.F.A Level II

Emphasis is placed on a rigorous and complete appraisal and evaluation of industries, companies and their common stocks as to current position and outlook, as well as to the investment implications of such an analysis for different investors. The candidate should be able to apply the techniques of security analysis, including measures for valuation and risk, to individual stocks and to companies within the same industry.

C.F.A Level III

Emphasis at this higher level is on the analysis and selection of common stocks, consistent with the financial circumstances of different types of individual and institutional investors and consistent with changing economic and market environments.

AREA SIX—PORTFOLIO MANAGEMENT
Pre-Candidate Requirements

Because the task of portfolio and investment management involves to a considerable extent the integration of economics, financial accounting, quantitative techniques, and security analysis, the pre-candidate requirements are the same as for those topic areas.

C.F.A. Preliminary Examination (C.F.A Level I)

The examinee is expected to understand the financial circumstances of different individual and institutional investors, to be able to formulate appropriate portfolio account objectives and constraints, and to be able to select specific investment instruments suitable for such portfolios.

C.F.A. Level II

At this level, the candidate should be able to construct portfolios and to formulate portfolio strategies based on an analysis of the outlook of the economy and of conditions in the securities markets. Emphasis is placed on security selection within the concepts of diversification, risk, return, and modern portfolio theory.

C.F.A. Level III

Based on knowledge gained at previous levels and in the other topic areas, the candidate is expected: (1) to interrelate economic and market conditions, securities analysis, analysis of the requirements of individual and institutional investors, and portfolio concepts; (2) to develop suitable investment policies; and (3) to construct appropriate portfolios. The candidate should have an understanding of the investment management process, including how to organize and implement the security analysis and portfolio management effort and how to evaluate the results.

AREA SEVEN—ETHICAL AND PROFESSIONAL STANDARDS
Pre-Candidate Requirements

Examinees are required to show evidence of sound character and to agree, in writing at the time of registration to abide by the I.C.F.A. *Code of Ethics, Standards of Professional Conduct*, and related rules. Character references are an integral part of the registration requirements. Violation of professional standards may result in suspension from the candidate program or revocation of the charter.

C.F.A. Preliminary Examination (C.F.A. Level I)

The examinee should be familiar with ethical and professional standards and security laws and regulations and should be able to deal with these standards as they pertain to his reponsibilities with the public, clients, employer, fellow analysts, and corporate managements.

C.F.A. Level II

The candidate should be able to recognize unprofessional practices and violations of standards in more sophisticated areas, including conflicts of interest and use of insider information, and to understand appropriate corrective actions.

C.F.A. Level III

The candidate should understand how to administer a program of professional and ethical standards within an organiztion in terms of internal disciplinary controls and of compliance with the I.C.F.A. standards and rules and with security laws and regulations. The candidate should understand the full meaning of the public interest, the professionalism of financial analysts, and ethical issues associated with changes in the financial systems.[4]

244 The C.F.A. Candidate Study Program—General Topic Outline

A general topic outline of the C.F.A. Candidate Study Program is shown in Exhibit 2-5.

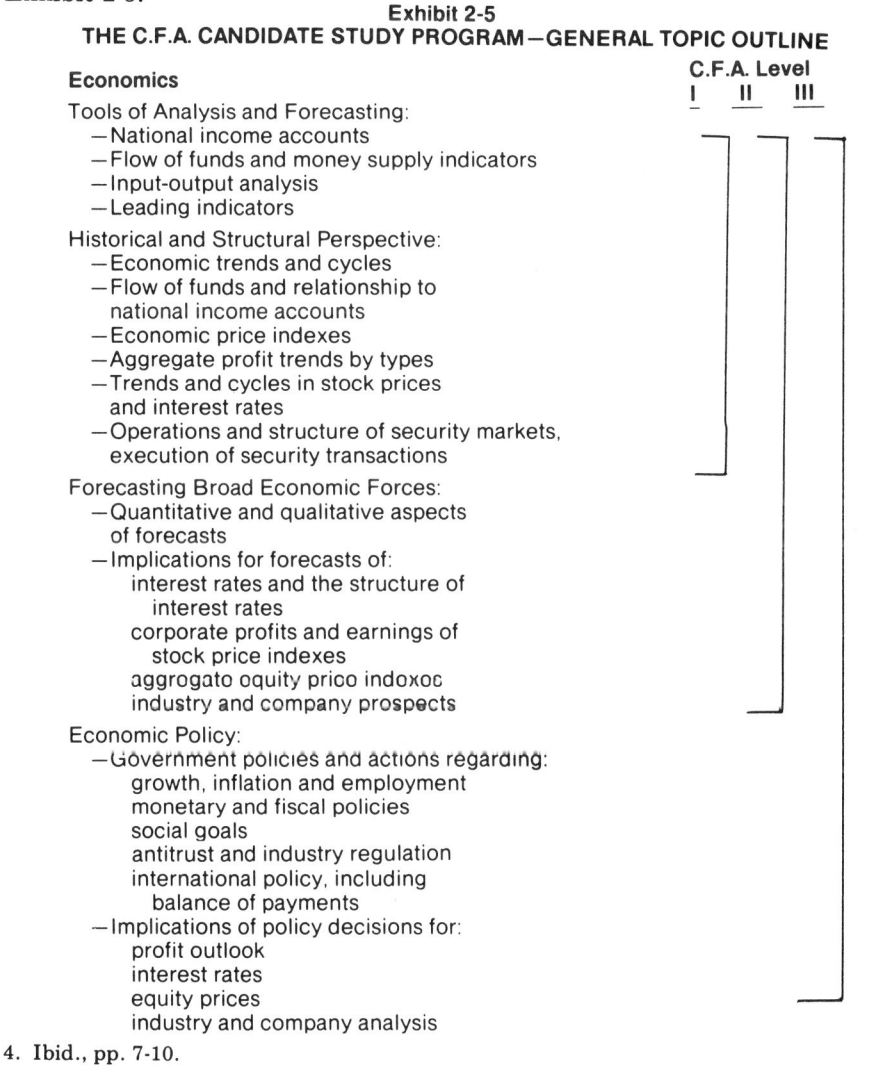

Exhibit 2-5
THE C.F.A. CANDIDATE STUDY PROGRAM—GENERAL TOPIC OUTLINE

Economics	C.F.A. Level I	II	III

Tools of Analysis and Forecasting:
—National income accounts
—Flow of funds and money supply indicators
—Input-output analysis
—Leading indicators

Historical and Structural Perspective:
—Economic trends and cycles
—Flow of funds and relationship to
   national income accounts
—Economic price indexes
—Aggregate profit trends by types
—Trends and cycles in stock prices
   and interest rates
—Operations and structure of security markets,
   execution of security transactions

Forecasting Broad Economic Forces:
—Quantitative and qualitative aspects
   of forecasts
—Implications for forecasts of:
   interest rates and the structure of
      interest rates
   corporate profits and earnings of
      stock price indexes
   aggregate equity price indexes
   industry and company prospects

Economic Policy:
—Government policies and actions regarding:
   growth, inflation and employment
   monetary and fiscal policies
   social goals
   antitrust and industry regulation
   international policy, including
      balance of payments
—Implications of policy decisions for:
   profit outlook
   interest rates
   equity prices
   industry and company analysis

---
4. Ibid., pp. 7-10.

Exhibit 2-5 (continued)

C.F.A. Level
I II III

Financial Accounting

Principles and Construction of
 Accounting Statements:
 —Income statements
 —Balance sheets
 —Sources and uses of funds

Content and Usefulness of Accounting
 Reports to Regulatory Agencies

Financial Analysis of Accounting
 Statements:
 —Adjustments for comparability
 —Ratio analysis
 —Adjustments for subsidiaries,
  affiliates and foreign operations
 —Stock splits and dividends
 —Rights, warrants and convertible
  securities
 —Effect of price level changes

Areas of Judgement:
 —Inventories
 —Depreciation
 —Tax treatment
 —Intangibles
 —Consolidation
 —Acquisitions and mergers
 —Deferred assets and liabilities
 —Off balance sheet financing
 —Pension plans

Current Accounting Principles and Practices:
 —AICPA and FASB opinions
 —Regulatory decisions

Application of Quantitative Techniques

Elementary Statistics:
 —Averages and measures of dispersion
Mathematics of Finance:
 —Compound growth
 —Present value of stocks and bonds
 —Performance measurement techniques

Probability Theory:
 —Expected values
 —Strategies
Hypothesis Testing:
 —Sample testing and confidence limits
 —Analysis of variance
Simple and Multiple Regression and
 Correlation
Matrix Algebra
Mathematical Programming in Portfolio
 Theory
Applications of Computer Systems to
 Financial Analysis

Exhibit 2-5 (continued)

                                                            C.F.A. Level
                                                                 I   II   III

**Techniques of Analysis—
Fixed-Income Securities**

Classification of Fixed Income Securities:
 —By issuer
 —By maturity, if any
 —By security
 —By contractual obligation
 —By tax status
 —Convertible features, if any
Special Characteristics:
 —Call features
 —Sinking fund provision
 —Security
 —Security
 —Protective covenants
 Taxable features

Fixed Income Security Selection and
Management:
 —Quality ratings
 —Interest or preferred dividend
    coverage, past and future
 —Coupon and Maturity
 —New issues, discount and premium bonds
 —The yield curve and interest rate structure
 —Marketability
 —Bond swaps

**Techniques of Analysis—
Equity Securities**

Sources of Information
Financial Instruments:
 —Stocks, warrants, rights, options

Industry Appraisal and Evaluation:
 —Interindustry competition, supply—demand
    product prices, costs and profits
 —Security market evaluation of profits,
    historical and projected

Company Appraisal and Evaluation:
 —Sales volume, product prices, product
    research, intraindustry competition
 —Ratio analysis balance sheet and income
    statement and analysis of corporte profit
    ability, liquidity, solvency, operting and
    financial leverage
 —Management appraisal
 —Earnings and dividend evaluation and
    projection, near and long-term
 —Valuation techniques-long and
    short-term:
        discounted cash flow
        earnings multiples, absolute and relative
        valuation models
        growth stock valuation
 —Risk analysis-quantitative and qualitative
 —Valuation analysis

Exhibit 2-5 (continued)

                                                              C.F.A. Level
                                                              I II III

**Objective of Analysis—
Portfolio Management**

Investor Objectives and Constraints:
— Individuals
— Institutions:
    investment companies
    foundations and endowment funds
    pension funds and profit sharing plans
    trust funds
    property and liability insurance
      companies
    life insurance companies
    commercial banks

Portfolio Strategy and Construction
— Policy inputs:
    assumptions regarding the short and
      long-term outlook for the economy
      and the securities markets
    types of investments to be used regard-
      ing quality, liquidity, risk and
      other characteristics
    portfolio diversification by type of
      investment and diversification
      by industry
— Account objectives and constraints:
    specific definition of objectives, e.g.,
      risk and return, liquidity require-
      ments, legal and regulatory constraints
    the time horizon for the investment
    aggressive and speculative properties
— Investment selection:
    selection of specific investments
      suitable for objectives
    comparative evaluation of alternative
      investments
— Modern portfolio theory and the construc-
  tion of "efficient portfolios"
— Tax planning
— Execution of purchases and sales
— Evaluation of account performance

Exhibit 2-5 (continued)

	C.F.A. Level
	I II III

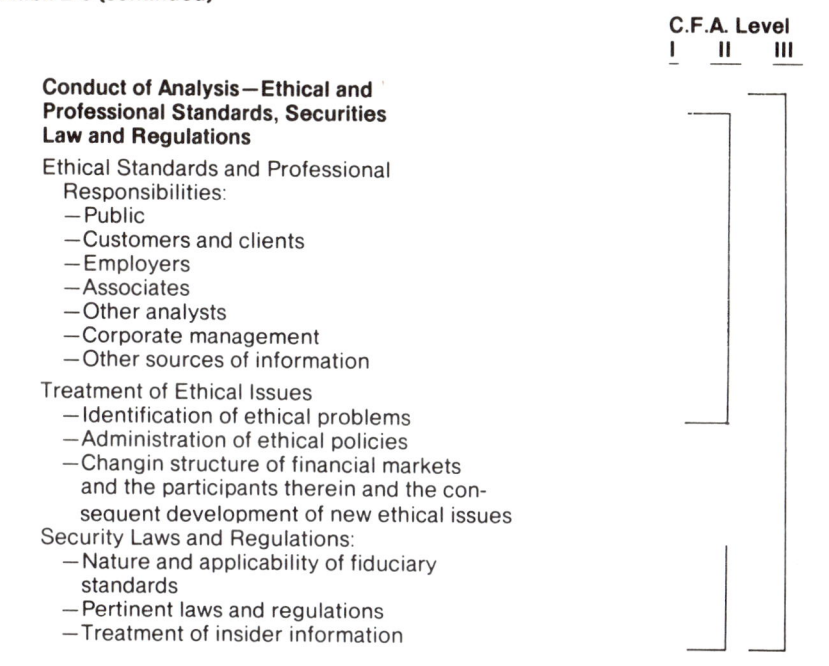

Conduct of Analysis—Ethical and Professional Standards, Securities Law and Regulations

Ethical Standards and Professional
  Responsibilities:
  —Public
  —Customers and clients
  —Employers
  —Associates
  —Other analysts
  —Corporate management
  —Other sources of information
Treatment of Ethical Issues
  —Identification of ethical problems
  —Administration of ethical policies
  —Changin structure of financial markets
    and the participants therein and the con-
    sequent development of new ethical issues
Security Laws and Regulations:
  —Nature and applicability of fiduciary
    standards
  —Pertinent laws and regulations
  —Treatment of insider information

Note: Reprinted from *The C.F.A. Announcement, 1977-78* (Charlottesville, Va.: The Institute of Chartered Financial Analysts, 1977), pp. 11-13.

245 Eligibility Requirements for C.F.A. Candidates

C.F.A. PRELIMINARY EXAMINATION
(C.F.A. LEVEL I)

Education Requirement: An examinee should have a bachelor's degree from an accredited academic institution. In the absence of a degree, other educational training or work experience may be accepted.

Occupation and Experience Requirement: There are no requirements. However acceptance as an examinee for and successful completion of the *C.F.A. Preliminary Examination (C.F.A. Level I)* does not necessarily mean that such examinee will be eligible for candidacy in the program at C.F.A. Level II and Level III. Each examination program has different eligibility requirements, as described below.

C.F.A. CANDIDATE LEVEL II

Occupation and Experience Requirement: The candidate must qualify under either A *or* B below:

A. As of August 1 preceding the year in which the examination is to be taken, the candidate must be primarily engaged in the occupation of financial analysis as related to investment securities as outlined on page 15 and as of this date must have completed *at least two years* of experience in one or more of these occuptional categories.

B. If *not currently* engaged in an eligible occupation as of August 1 preceding the year in which the examination is to be taken, the candidate must have been primarily engaged, for *at least four years,* in the occupation of financial analysis as related to investment securities.

Society Membership Requirement: A candidate must be a member in good standing of a constituent society of The Financial Analysts Federation. Membership in a constituent society must be obtained by *April 15* of the year in which the examination is to be taken. It is the *Candidate's* responsibility to report his (her) membership to the Institute.

C.F.A. CANDIDATE LEVEL III

Occupation and Experience Requirement: The candidate must qualify under either A *or* B below:

A. As of August 1 preceding the year in which the examination is to be taken, the candidate must be primarily engaged in the occupation of financial analysis as related to investment securities as outlined on page 15 and as of this date must have completed *at least three years* of experience in one or more of these occupational categories. The candidate must complete *at least four years* of experience prior to the award of the C.F.A. **designation.**

B. If not currently engaged in an eligible occupation as of August 1 preceding the year in which the examination is to be taken, the candidate must have been primarily engaged, for *at least four years,* in the occupation of financial analysis as related to investment securities.

Society Membership Requirement: A candidate must be a member in good standing of a constituent society of the Financial Analysts Federation.[5]

246 C.F.A. Candidate Application Procedures and Forms

Additional information concerning the C.F.A. Candidate Study Program and the Examination Series as well as registration and enrollment application forms may be obtained by writing:

> The Registrar
> The Institute of Chartered Financial Analysts
> University of Virginia
> Post Office Box 3668
> Charlottesville, Virginia 22903

5. Ibid., p. 14.

3
Accounting Literature

310 OFFICIAL LITERATURE IN FINANCIAL ACCOUNTING

The Council of the AICPA in 1964 recognized all effective *Accounting Research Bulletins* and *Opinions of the Accounting Principles Board (APB)* to be substantial authoritative support for generally accepted accounting principles. It further ruled that subsequent to 1965, all departures from such releases by its members were to be disclosed via footnote in financial statements or within audit reports.

Upon the inception of the Financial Accounting Standards Board (FASB) in 1973, the Council reaffirmed its prior ruling, recognizing FASB *Statements of Financial Accounting Standards* together with those *Accounting Research Bulletins (ARB's)* and *APB Opinions* not superseded by subsequent FASB action, to embody generally accepted accounting principles. As such, all are within the realm of Rule 203 ("Rules of Conduct," *Code of Professional Ethics).*

311 Accounting Research and Terminology Bulletins—AICPA

These were the pronouncements of the AICPA issued during the period 1939 to 1959 by the Committee on Accounting Procedure and the Committee on Terminology, prior to the creation of the Accounting Principles Board. A total of forty-two bulletins were issued between 1939 and 1953. Of these first bulletins, eight were released by the Committee on Terminology and were subsequently published in 1953 as *Accounting Terminology Bulletin No. 1.* The remaining thirty-four bulletins were revised the same year (with three being omitted due to their lack of relevancy by 1953) and released as *Accounting Research Bulletin No. 43* by the Committee on Accounting Procedure.

Accounting Research Bulletins

No. 43   *Restatement and Revision of Accounting Research Bulletins,* 1953
No. 44   *Declining-Balance Depreciation,* 1954 (revised 1958)
No. 45   *Long-Term Construction-Type Contracts,* 1955
No. 46   *Discontinuance of Dating Earned Surplus,* 1956
No. 47   *Accounting for Costs of Pension Plans,* 1956
No. 48   *Business Combinations,* 1957
No. 49   *Earnings per Share,* 1958
No. 50   *Contingencies,* 1958
No. 51   *Consolidated Financial Statements,* 1959

Accounting Terminology Bulletins

No. 1 *Review and Resume,* 1953
No. 2 *Proceeds, Revenue, Income, Profit, and Earnings,* 1955
No. 3 *Book Value,* 1956
No. 4 *Cost, Expense and Loss,* 1957

312 Opinions of the APB—AICPA

These were the official pronouncements of the Accounting Principles Board during the period 1959 through 1973.

No. 1 *New Depreciation Guidelines and Rules,* 1962
No. 2 *Accounting for the "Investment Credit,"* 1962
No. 3 *The Statement of Sources and Application of Funds,* 1963
No. 4 *Accounting for the "Investment Credit,"* 1964
No. 5 *Reporting of Leases in Financial Statements of Lessee,* 1964
No. 6 *Status of Accounting Research Bulletins,* 1965
No. 7 *Accounting for Leases in Financial Statements of Lessors,* 1966
No. 8 *Accounting for the Cost of Pension Plans,* 1966
No. 9 *Reporting the Results of Operations,* 1966
No. 10 *Omnibus Opinion—1966,* 1966
No. 11 *Accounting for Income Taxes,* 1967
No. 12 *Omnibus Opinion—1967,* 1967
No. 13 *Amending Paragraph 6 of APB Opinion No. 9, Application to Commercial Banks,* 1969
No. 14 *Accounting for Convertible Debt Issued with Stock Purchase Warrants,* 1969
No. 15 *Earnings per Share,* 1969
No. 16 *Business Combinations,* 1970
No. 17 *Intangible Assets,* 1970
No. 18 *The Equity Method of Accounting for Investments in Common Stock,* 1971
No. 19 *Reporting Changes in Financial Position,* 1971
No. 20 *Accounting Changes,* 1971
No. 21 *Interest on Receivables and Payables,* 1971
No. 22 *Disclosure of Accounting Policies,* 1971
No. 23 *Accounting for Income Taxes—Special Areas,* 1972
No. 24 *Accounting for Income Taxes—Investments in Common Stock Accounted for by the Equity Method (Other than Subsidiaries and Corporate Joint Ventures),* 1972
No. 25 *Accounting for Stock Issued to Employees,* 1972
No. 26 *Early Extinguishment of Debt,* 1972
No. 27 *Accounting for Lease Transactions by Manufacturer or Dealer Lessors,* 1972
No. 28 *Interim Financial Reporting,* 1973

No. 29   *Accounting for Nonmonetary Transactions,* 1973
No. 30   *Reporting the Results of Operations,* 1973
No. 31   *Disclosure of Lease Commitments by Lessees,* 1973

313 Statements of the FASB

Statements of Financial Accounting Standards are the official pronouncements of the organization currently empowered to issue statements on corporate financial reporting that are within the realm of Rule 203 of the *Code of Professional Ethics.* Definitive pronoucements as of late 1977 follow:

Statements

No. 1   *Disclosure of Foreign Currency Translation Information,* December 1973
No. 2   *Accounting for Research and Development Costs,* October 1974
No. 3   *Reporting Accounting Changes in Interim Financial Statements,* December 1974
No. 4   *Reporting Gains and Losses from Extinguishment of Debt,* March 1975
No. 5   *Accounting for Contingencies,* March 1975
No. 6   *Classification of Short-Term Obligations Expected to be Refinanced,* May 1975
No. 7   *Accounting and Reporting by Development Stage Enterprises,* June 1975
No. 8   *Accounting for the Translation of Foreign Currency Transactions and Foreign Currency Financial Statements,* October 1975
No. 9   *Accounting for Income Taxes—Oil and Gas Producing Companies,* October 1975
No. 10 *Extension of "Grandfather," Provisions for Business Combinations,* October 1975
No. 11 *Accounting for Contingencies—Transition Method,* December 1975
No. 12 *Accounting for Certain Marketable Securities,* December 1975
No. 13 *Accounting for Leases,* November 1976
No. 14 *Financial Reporting for Segments of a Business Enterprise,* December 1976
No. 15 *Accounting by Debtors and Creditors or Troubled Debt Restructurings,* June 1977
No. 16 **Prior Period Adjustments,** June 1977

Interpretations

No. 1   *Accounting Changes Related to the Cost of Inventory* (APB Opinion No. 20), June 1974
No. 2   *Imputing Interest on Debt Arrangements Made under the Federal Bankruptcy Act* (APB Opinion No. 21), June 1974

No. 3   *Accounting for the Cost of Pension Plans Subject to the Employee Retirement Income Security Act of 1974* (APB Opinion No. 8), December 1974
No. 4   *Applicability of FASB Statement No. 2 to Business Combinations Accounted for by the Purchase Method,* February 1975
No. 5   *Applicability of FASB Statement No. 2 to Development Stage Enterprises,* February 1975
No. 6   *Applicability of FASB Statement No. 2 to Computer Software,* February 1975
No. 7   *Applying FASB Statement No. 7 in Financial Statements of Established Operating Enterprises,* October 1975
No. 8   *Classification of a Short-Term Obligation Repaid Prior to Being Replaced by a Long-Term Security* (FASB Statement No. 6), January 1976
No. 9   *Applying APB Opinions No. 16 and 17 when a Savings and Loan Association or a Similar Institution is Acquired in a Business Combination Accounted for by the Purchase Method,* February 1976
No. 10 *Application of FASB Statement No. 12 to Personal Financial Statements* (FASB Statement No. 12), September 1976
No. 11 *Changes in Market Value after the Balance Sheet Date* (FASB Statement No. 12), September 1976
No. 12 *Accounting for Previously Established Allowance Accounts* (FASB Statement No. 12), September 1976
No. 13 *Consolidation of a Parent and Its Subsidiaries Having Different Balance Sheet Dates* (FASB Statement No. 12), September 1976
No. 14 *Reasonable Estimation of the Amount of a Loss* (FASB Statement No. 5), September 1976
No. 15 *Translation of Unamortized Policy Acquisition Costs by a Stock Life Insurance Company* (FASB Statement No. 8), September 1976
No. 16 *Clarification of Definitions and Accounting for Marketable Equity Securities that Become Non-Marketable* (FASB Statement No. 12), February 1977
No. 17 *Applying the Lower of Cost or Market Rule in Translated Financial Statements* (FASB Statement No. 8), February 1977
No. 18 *Accounting for Income Taxes in Interim Periods,* March 1977

314 SEC Accounting Series Releases

SEC releases, consisting of the SEC's interpretations of its accounting rules and regulations, are issued as necessary by the SEC. As of late 1977 there were 210 such releases. A compilation of the first 112 releases is available from the U.S. Government Printing Office and later releases may be obtained directly from the SEC.

315 CASB Standards

The CASB (Cost Accounting Standards Board) was created by an act of Congress in 1970 through an amendment of the Defense Production Act of 1950. Its purpose was to deal with the cost accounting problems often associated with significant negotiated government contracts. By late 1977 the CASB had issued fifteen standards as follows:

No. 401 *Consistency in Estimating, Accumulating and Reporting Cost,* 1972
No. 402 *Consistency in Allocating Costs Incurred for the Same Purpose,* 1972
No. 403 *Allocation of Home Office Expenses to Segments,* 1973
No. 404 *Capitalization of Tangible Assets,* 1973
No. 405 *Accounting For Unallowable Costs,* 1973
No. 406 *Cost Accounting Period,* 1974
No. 407 *Use of Standard Costs for Direct Material and Direct Labor,* 1974
No. 408 *Accounting for Costs of Compensated Personal Absense,* 1974
No. 409 *Depreciation of Tangible Capital Assets,* 1975
No. 410 *Allocation of G&A Expense,* 1975
No. 411 *Accounting for Acquisition Cost of Material,* 1976
No. 412 *Composition and Measurement of Pension Costs,* 1976
No. 413 (Withdrawn)
No. 414 *Cost of Money as an Element of the Cost of Facilities,* 1976
No. 415 *Accounting for the Cost of Deferred Compensation,* 1976

320 ACCOUNTING RESEARCH STUDIES—AICPA

The *Accounting Research Studies,* authored by independent researchers or by members of the Accounting Research Division of the AICPA, were *not* official pronouncements of the Institute. However, because they did represent concentrated study in specific problem areas in financial accounting, they frequently led to official pronoucements.

No. 1 *The Basic Postulates of Accounting,* by Maurice Moonitz, 1961
No. 2 *"Cash Flow" Analysis and the Funds Statement,* by Perry Mason, 1961
No. 3 *A Tentative Set of Broad Accounting Principles for Business Enterprises,* by Robert T. Sprouse and Maurice Moonitz, 1962
No. 4 *Reporting of Leases in Financial Statements,* by John H. Myers, 1962
No. 5 *A Critical Study of Accounting for Business Combinations,* by Arthur R. Wyatt, 1963
No. 6 *Reporting Financial Effects of Price-Level Changes,* by staff, 1963

No. 7 *Inventory of Generally Accepted Accounting Principles for Business Enterprises,* by Paul Grady, 1965
No. 8 *Accounting for the Cost of Pension Plans,* by Ernest L. Hicks, 1965
No. 9 *Interperiod Allocation of Corporate Income Taxes,* by Homer Black, 1966
No. 10 *Accounting for Goodwill,* by George R. Catlett and Norman O. Olson, 1966
No. 11 *Financial Reporting in the Extractive Industries,* by Robert E. Field, 1969
No. 12 *Reporting Foreign Operations of U.S. Companies in U.S. Dollars,* by Leonard Lorensen, 1972
No. 13 *The Accounting Basis of Inventories,* by Horace G. **Barden,** 1973
No. 14 *Accounting for Research and Development Expenditures,* by Oscar S. Gellein and Maurice S. Newman, 1973
No. 15 *Stockholders' Equity,* by Beatrice Melcher, 1973

330 STATEMENTS OF THE APB—AICPA

During the period 1962 to 1970, four statements, primarily informative in nature, were issued as special reports on specific areas of interest in financial accounting.

No. 1 *Statement by the Accounting Principles Board,* 1962
No. 2 *Disclosure of Supplemental Financial Information by Diversified Companies,* 1967
No. 3 *Financial Statements Restated for General Price-Level Changes,* 1969
No. 4 *Basic Concepts and Accounting Principles Underlying* **Financial Statements** *of Business Enterprises,* 1970

340 AUDITING LITERATURE

In the United States the AICPA has been primarily responsible for standards governing public auditing. The official statements on auditing procedures and standards have been released in the form of *Statements on Auditing Procedure* and *Statements on Auditing Standards* by the AICPA.

341 Statements on Auditing Procedure—AICPA

These statements were issued by the Committee on Auditing Procedure of the AICPA from 1939 to 1972 and represented attempts by the Institute to set forth auditing guidelines for the independent auditor. A **total of fifty-four such statements were released;** however, No. 33, published in 1963, **was essentially a codification of the preceding thirty-two statements.**

342 Statements on Auditing Standards—AICPA

In 1973 the Committee on Auditing Procedure released the first in the currrent series of official AICPA auditing guidelines for independent auditors. It represented a codification of Statements on Auditng Procedures Nos. 33 through 54 previously issued. Statements subsequent to Statement on Auditng Standards No. 1 have been released by the Auditing Standards Executive Committee of the AICPA. The subject matter and date of those releases follows:

No. 1 *Codification of Auditing Standards and Procedures,* November 1972
No. 2 *Reports on Audited Financial Statements,* October 1974
No. 3 *The Effects of EDP on the Auditor's Study and Evaluation of Internal Control,* December 1974
No. 4 *Quality Contol Considerations for a Firm of Independent Auditors,* December 1974
No. 5 *The Meaning of "Present Fairly in Conformity with Generally Accepted Accounting Principles" in the Independent Auditor's Report,* July 1975
No. 6 *Related Party Transactions,* July 1975
No. 7 **Communications Between Predecessor and Successor Auditors,** October 1975
No. 8 *Other Information in Documents Containing Audited Financial Statements,* December 1975
No. 9 *The Effect of an Internal Audit Function on the Scope of the Independent Auditor's Examination,* December 1975
No. 10 *Limited Review of Interim Financial Information,* December 1975
No. 11 *Using the Work of a Specialist,* December 1975
No. 12 *Inquiry of a Client's Lawyer Concerning Litigation, Claims, and Assessments,* January 1976
No. 13 *Reports on Limited Review of Interim Financial Information,* May 1976
No. 14 *Special Reports,* December 1976
No. 15. *Reports on Comparative Financial Statements,* December 1976
No. 16 *The Independent Auditor's Responsibility for the Detection of Errors or Irregularities,* January 1977
No. 17 *Illegal Acts of Clients,* January 1977
No. 18 *Unaudited Replacement Cost Information,* **May 1977**
No. 19 *Client Representations,* June 1977
No. 20 Required Communication of Material Weaknesses in Internal Accounting Control, August, 1977

350 AMERICAN ACCOUNTING ASSOCIATION PUBLICATIONS

Since its establishment in 1916, the American Accounting Association (AAA) has made several valuable contributions to the field of accounting literature. In addition to the individual publications of its members, the several committees of the AAA have issued basic statements and committee reports in furtherance of the organization's goals—namely, to encourage and support research and to seek the development and acceptance of accounting principles and standards.

Following is a representative collection of AAA publications:

Accounting and Reporting Standards for Corporate Financial Statements, 1957 revision

    Originally issued in 1936 as *A Tentative Statement of Accounting Principles Underlying Corporate Financial Statements*

    Revised in 1941 by *Accounting Principles Underlying Corporate Financial Statements*

    Revised again in 1946 as *Accounting Concepts and Standards Underlying Corporate Financial Statements*

Accounting Education Series, Nos, 1-2.

    No. 1 *Accounting Education: Problems and Prospects*, by James Don Edwards, ed.

    No. 2 *Researching the Accounting Curriculum: Strategies for Change*, by William Ferrara, ed.

Monograph Series, Nos. 1-7 (1937-1965).

    No. 1 *Principles of Public Utility Depreciation*, by Perry Mason (out-of-print)

    No. 2 *Financial Statements*, by M.B. Daniels (o.p.)

    No. 3 *An Introduction to Corporate Accounting Standards*, by W.A. Paton and A.C. Littleton

    No. 4 *The Entity Theory of Consolidated Statements*, by Maurice Moonitz (o.p.)

    No. 5 *Structure of Accounting Theory*, by A.C. Littleton

    No. 6 *The Philosophy of Auditing*, by R.K. Mautz and H.A. Sharaf

    No. 7 *An Inquiry into the Nature of Accounting*, by Louis Goldberg (o.p.)

A Statement of Basic Accounting Theory, 1966 (supercedes the 1957 revision)

Studies in Accounting Research, Nos. 1-10, 1969—

    No. 1 *Investment Analysis and General Price-Level Adjustments: A Behavioral Study*, by Thomas R. Dyckman

    No. 2 *Accounting and Information Theory*, by Baruch Lev

No. 3 *The Allocation Problem in Financial Accounting*, by Arthur Lawrence **Thomas**
No. 4 *Accounting Controls and the Soviet Economic Reforms of 1966*, by Bertrand Horwitz
No. 5 *Information Evaluation*, by Gerald A. Feltham
No. 6 *A Statement of Basic Auditing Concepts*, by the Committee of Basic Auditing **Concepts.**
No. 7 *Valuation of Used Capital Assets*, by Carl Beidleman
No. 8 *Obtaining Agreement on Standards in the Accounting Profession*, by Maurice Moonitz
No. 9 *The Allocation Problem; Part Two*, by Arthur Lawrence Thomas
No. 10 *Theory of Accounting Measurement*, by Yuji Ijiri

Zeff, Stephen A. *The American Accounting Association: Its First Fifty Years*. Evanston, Ill.: AAA, 1966.

360 JOURNALS IN ACCOUNTING

Journals and other periodicals play an important role in the dynamic field of accounting. It is through the periodical literature that the accountant keeps pace with new developments. Although there are currently many periodicals in the accounting area published throughout the world, the following list contains only those in the English language which are generrlly available in most university libraries. This list is by no means exhaustive.

Abacus. Sydney University Press, Press Building, University of Sydney, New South Wales 2006, Australia.
Accountancy. Institute of Chartered Accountants in England and Wales, 56-66 Goswell Road, London ELIM 7AB England.
The Accountant. Gee & Co. Ltd., 151 Strand, London W.C.2 **England.**
Accountants' Journal. New Zealand Society of Accountants, Box 10046, Wellington, New Zealand.
The Accounting Review. American Accounting Association, 653 South Orange Avenue, Sarasota, Florida 33577.
Australian Accountant. Australian Society of Accountants, 49 Exhibition Street, Melbourne 3000, Australia.
Canadian Chartered Accountant. Canadian Institute of Chartered Accountants, 250 Bloor Street, E., Toronto 5, Ontario, Canada.
Chartered Accountants in Australia. Institute of Chartered Accountants in Australia, Box 3921, G.P.O., Sydney 2001, Australia.
The CPA Journal. New York State Society of Certified Public Accountants, 600 Third Avenue, New York, New York 10016.
Federal Accountant. Federal Government Accountants Association, 727 South 23rd Street, Arlington, Virginia 22202.

Financial Executive. Financial Executives Institute, 633 Third Avenue, New York, New York 10017.

The Internal Auditor. Institute of Internal Auditors, 170 Broadway, New York, New York 10038.

International Journal of Accounting Education and Research. Center for International Education and Research in Accounting, 320 Commerce West, University of Illinois, Urbana, Illinois 61801.

Journal of Accountancy. American Institute of Certified Public Accountants, 1211 Avenue of the Americas, New York, New York 10036.

Journal of Accounting Research. Institute of Professional Accounting, Graduate School of Business, University of Chicago, Chicago, Illinois, 60637.

Management Accounting. National Association of Accountants, 919 Third Avenue, New York, New York 10022.

The Practical Accountant. The Institute for Continuing Professional Development, 964 Third Avenue, New York, New York 10022.

The Tax Executive. Tax Executives Institute, Inc., 425 13th Street, N.W., Washington, D.C. 20004.

Taxation for Accountants. The Journal of Taxation, Ltd. 512 North Florida Ave., Tampa, Florida 33602.

The Woman CPA. American Woman's Society of Certified Public Accountants, and The American Society of Women Accountants, Suite 1036, 35 E. Wacker Drive, Chicago, Illinois 60601.

370 TEXTS AND GENERAL REFERENCES

This section includes some of the useful and popular general references in accounting. It is not an exhaustive list of the literature.

371 General Works

American Institute of Certified Public Accountants. *Accountants' Index.* New York: AICPA, 1921. Supplements, 1923-.

Accounting Trends and Techniques. New York: AICPA, 1948-.

Davidson, Sidney, James S. Schindler, Clyde P. Stickney, and Roman L. Weil, *Accounting: The Language of Business.* Glen Ridge, N.J.: Thomas Horton and Daughters, 1977.

Demarest, Rosemary R. *Accounting Information Sources.* Detroit: Gale Research Co., 1970.

Dickey, Robert I. *Accountants' Cost Handbook.* 5th ed. New York: Ronald Press Co., 1970.

Federal Government Accountants Association. *Bibliography on Federal Accounting, Auditing, Budgeting, and Reporting 1900-1970* (annotated). Arlington, Va.: Federal Government Accountants Association, 1971.

Kohler, Eric Louis. *Dictionary for Accountants.* 5th ed. Englewood Cliffs, N.J.: Prentice-Hall, 1975.

Lipkin, Lawrence, Irwin K. Feinstein, and Lucile Derrick. *Accountant's Handbook of Formulas and Tables.* 2d ed. Englewood Cliffs, N.J.: Prentice-Hall, 1973.

May, Robert, et al. *A Brief Introduction to Managerial and Social Uses of Accounting,* Englewood Cliffs, N.J.: Prentice-Hall, 1975.

Prentice-Hall Editorial Staff, *Accountants' Encyclopedia. 4 vols.* Englewood Cliffs, N.J.: Prentice-Hall, 1965.

Price-Waterhouse & Co. *Thesaurus of Accounting and Auditing Terminology.* New York: Price-Waterhouse & Co., 1974.

Roy, Robert H., and James H. McNeil. *Horizons for a Profession: The Common Body of Knowledge for Certified Public Accountants.* New York: AICPA, 1967.

Wixon, Rufus, Walter G. Kell, and Norton M. Bedford, editorial consultants. *Accountants' Handbook.* 5th ed. New York: Ronald Press Co., 1970.

372 Accounting History

Briloff, Abraham J. *Unaccountable Accounting.* New York: Harper & Row, 1972.

Brown, Richard. *History of Accounting & Accountants* (Repr. of 1905 ed.) Clifton, N.J.: Kelley.

Brown, R.Gene, and Kenneth S. Johnson. *Pacioli on Accounting.* New York. McGraw-Hill, 1963.

Burns, Thomas J. *Accounting in Transition: Oral Histories of Recent U.S. Experience.* Columbus, Ohio: Ohio State University Press, 1974.

Carey, John L. *The Rise of the Accounting Profession.* 2 vols. New York AICPA, 1970.

Chatfield, Michael. *Contemporary Studies in the Evolution of Accounting Thought.* Belmont, California.: Dickenson, 1968.

Deinzer, Harvey T. *Development of Accounting Thought.* New York: Holt, Rinehart & Winston, 1965.

Edwards, James Don. *History of Public Accounting in the United States* East Lansing, Mich.: Michigan State University Press, 1960.

Edwards, James Don, and Roland F. Salmonson. *Contributions of Four Accounting Pioneers: Kohler, Littleton, May, Paton.* East Lansing, Mich.: Michigan State University Press, 1961.

Garner, S. Paul. *Evolution of Cost Accounting to 1925.* University, Ala.: University of Alabama Press, 1954.

Littleton, A.C. *Accounting Evolution to 1900.* New York: American Institute Publishing Co., 1933.

Littleton, A.C. and B.S. Yamey. *Studies in the History of Accounting.* London: Sweet & Maxwell, Ltd., 1956.

Moonitz, Maurice, and A.C. Littleton. *Significant Accounting Essays.* Englewood Cliffs, N.J.: Prentice-Hall, 1965.

Woolf, Arthur H. *A History of Accountants & Accountancy.* New York: Gordon Press.

373 Financial Accounting Theory

American Institute of Certified Public Accountants. *Objectives of Financial statements.* New York: AICPA, 1973.

Backer, Morton, ed. *Modern Accounting Theory.* Englewood Cliffs, N.J.: Prentice-Hall, 1966.

Chatfield, Michael. *Contemporary Studies in the Evolution of Accounting Thought.* Belmont, Calif.: Dickenson, 1968.

Davidson, Sidney, et. al., ed. *An Income Approach to Accounting Theory.* Englewood Cliffs, N.J.: Prentice-Hall, 1964.

Financial Accounting Standards Board. Financial Accounting Standards. Chicago: Commerce Clearing House, 1975.

Gilman, Stephen. *Accounting Concepts of Profit.* New York: Ronald Press, 1939.

Hendriksen, Eldon S. *Accounting Theory* 3rd ed. Homewood, Ill.: Richard D. Irwin, 1977.

Ijiri, Yuji. *The Foundtions of Accounting Measurement: A Mathematical, Economic and Behavioral Inquiry.* Englewood Cliffs, N.J.: Prentice-Hall, 1967.

Littleton, A.C., and V.K. Zimmerman. *Accounting Theory: Continuity and Change.* Englewood Cliffs, N.J.: Prentice-Hall, 1962.

Moonitz, Maurice. *The Basic Postulates of Accounting.* Accounting Research Study No. 1. New York: AICPA, 1961.

Paton, William A., and A.C. Littleton. *An Introduction to Corporate Accounting Standards.* AAA Monograph No. 3. Madison, Wis. AAA, 1940 (reprinted 1962).

Salmonson, Roland F. *Basic Financial Accounting Theory.* Belmont, Calif.: Wadsworth, 1969.

Sprouse, Robert T., and Maurice Moonitz. *A Tentative Set of Broad Accounting Principles for Business Enterprises.* Accounting Research Study No. 3. New York: AICPA, 1962.

Stone, Willard E. *Foundations of Accounting Theory.* Gainesvile, Fla.: University of Florida Press, 1973.

Zeff, Stephen A., and Thomas F. Keller, eds. *Financial Accounting Theory No. 1: Issues and Controversies.* New York: McGraw-Hill, 1973.

374 Cost and Managerial

Bierman, Harold, Jr., and Thomas R. Dyckman. *Managerial Cost Accounting.* 2d ed. New York: Macmillan, 1976.

Copeland, Benny R., and Nelson G. Sullivan. *Cost Accounting: Accumulation, Analysis, and Control.* St. Paul, Minn.: West, 1977.

Crowningshield, Gerald R., and Kenneth Gorman. *Cost Accounting: Principles and Managerial Applications.* 3rd ed. Boston: Houghton Mifflin, 1974.

Dopuch, Nicholas, and Jacob G. Birnberg. *Cost Accounting: Accounting Data for Management's Decisions.* 2d ed. New York: Harcourt Brace Jovanovich, 1974.

Horngren, Charles T. *Accounting in Management Control : An Introduction.* 3d ed. Englewood Cliffs, N.J.: Prentice-Hall, 1974.
Cost Accounting: A Managerial Emphasis. 4th ed. Engelwood Cliffs, N.J.: Prentice-Hall, 1976.

Matz, Adolph, and O.J. Curry. *Cost Accounting: Planning and Control.* 6th ed. Cincinnati: South-Western, 1976.

Moore, Carl L. and Robert K. Jaedicke. *Managerial Accounting*, 4th ed. Cincinnati: South-Western, 1976.

Shillinglaw, Gordon. *Cost Accounting: Analysis and Control.* 3rd ed. Homewood, Ill.: Richard D. Irwin, 1972.

Thacker, Ronald J. and Richard L. Smith, *Modern Management Accounting*, Reston, Va.: Reston Publishing Co., 1976.

375 Tax

American Institute of Certified Public Accountants. *Accountants Tax Practice Management Handbook.* New York: AICPA 1974.

Bittker, Boris I., and James S. Eustice. *Federal Income Taxation of Corporations and Shareholders.* 3d ed. Boston: Warren, Gorham & Lamont

Committee for Economic Development. *A Better Balance in Federal Taxes in Business.* New York: Committee on Economic Development, 1966.

Crumley, D. Larry, and P. Michael Davis. *Organizing, Operating and Terminating Subchapter S Corporation,* Tucson, Ariz.: Lawyers and Judges Publishing Co., 1974.

Federal Tax Return Manual. Chicago, Commerce Clearing House.

Gray, Otto L. *New Directions in Collegiate Tax Offerings? Opinions of Tax Professors.* Research Monogram No. 27. Atlanta: Georgia State University Press, 1963.

Hoffman, William H., ed., *West's Federal Taxation: Corportions, Partnerships, Estates and Trusts.* St. Paul, Minn.: West, 1977.

Hohenstein, Henry. *The IRS Conspiracy.* Freeport, N.Y.: Nash Publishing Co., New York: 1974.

Meyers, Edward M., and John J. Urban. *Incentive Tax Credits.* New York: Praeger, 1974.

Phillips, Lawrence C. and William H. Hoffman, eds., *West's Federal Taxation: Individual.* St. Paul, Minn.: West, 1978.

Prentice-Hall Federal Tax Course. Englewood Cliffs, N.J.: Prentice-Hall, published annually.

Raby, William L. *The Income Tax and Business Decisions: An Introduction to Federal Taxes for Accountants and Managers.* 3d. ed. Englewood Cliffs, N.J.: Prentice-Hall, 1975.

Sommerfield, Ray M. *Federal Taxes and Management Decisions.* Homewood, Ill.: Richard D. Irwin, 1974.

Storich, A. *How to Build a More Lucrative Tax Practice.* Englewood Cliffs, N.J.: Prentice-Hall, 1970.

Tax Services

Cavitch, Zolman. *Tax Planning for Corporations and Shareholders.* New York: M. Bender.

Federal Taxes. Englewood Cliffs, N.J.: Prentice-Hall.

Mertens, Jacob. *The Law of Federal Income Taxation.* Chicago: Callaghan & Co.

Rabkins, Jacob, and Mark Johnson. *Federal Income, Gift, and Estate Taxation.* New York: M. Bender.

Standard Federal Tax Reports. Chicago: Commerce Clearing House.

Tax Coordinator. New York: Tax Research Institute of America.

Tax Management Portfolios for Executives. Washington, D.C.: Bureau of National Affairs.

376 Auditing

American Institute of Certified Public Accountants. *An Auditor's Approach to Statistical Sampling,* No. 1-. New York: AICPA, 1967-.
　　Case Studies in Auditing Procedure. No. 1-. New York: AICPA, 1947-.
　　Industry Audit Guides. New York: AICPA, 1956-.

Arkin, Herbert. *Handbook of Sampling for Auditing and Accounting.* 2d ed. New York: McGraw-Hill, 1974.

Boutell, Wayne S., ed. *Contemporary Auditing.* Belmont, Calif.: Dickenson, 1970.

Brasseaux, Herman, and Francis L. Miles. *Auditor's Report: A Book of Cases.* 1st ed. Cincinnati: South-Western, 1972.

Carmichael, Douglas R., and John J. Willingham. *Perspectives in Auditing.* Text ed. New York: McGraw-Hill, 1975.
Cashin, James A. *Handbook for Auditors.* New York: McGraw-Hill, 1971.
Davis, Gordon B. *Auditing and EDP.* New York: AICPA, 1968.
Defliese, P.L. *Montgomery's Auditing.* 9th ed. New York: Ronald Press Co., 1975.
Holmes, Arthur W. *Basic Auditing Principles.* 4th ed. Homewood, Ill.: Richard D. Irwin, 1972.
Meigs, Walter B., E. John Larsen, and Robert F. Meigs. *Principles of Auditing.* 5th ed. Homewood, Ill.: Richard D. Irwin, 1973.
Porter, W. Thomas, Jr., and John C. Burton. *Auditing: A Conceptual Approach.* Belmont, Calif.: Wadsworth, 1971.
Sawyer, Lawrence B. *The Practice of Modern Internal Auditing: Appraising Operations for Management.* New York: Institute of Internal Auditors, 1973.
Stettler, Howard F. *Systems Based Independent Audits.* 2d ed. Englewood Cliffs, N.J.: Prentice-Hall, 1974.
Willingham, John J., and D.R. Carmichael. *Auditing Concepts and Methods.* 2d ed. New York: McGraw-Hill, 1975.
Woods, Richard S., ed. *Audit Decisions in Accounting Practice.* New York: Ronald Press Co., 1973.

377 Quantitative Methods; Systems; Computers

Ackoff, Russel L., and Maurice W. Sasieni. *Fundamentals of Operations Research.* New York: Wiley & Sons, 1968.
American Institute of Certified Public Accountants. *Accounting and the Computer.* New York: AICPA, 1966.
Bierman, Harold, et al. *Quantitative Analysis for Business Decisions.* 4th ed. Homewood, Ill.: Richard D. Irwin, 1973.
Boutell, Wayne S. *Computer Oriented Business Systems.* 2d ed. Englewood Cliffs, N.J.: Prentice-Hall 1973.
Byrkit, Donald R. *Elements of Statistics.* New York: D. Van Nostrand, 1975.
Davis, Gordon B. *Introduction to Management Information Systems: Conceptual Foundations, Structure and Development.* New York: McGraw-Hill, 1974.
Hein, Leonard W., ed. *Contemporary Accounting and the Computer.* Belmont, Calif.: Dickenson, 1969.
Hughes, Ann, and Dennis E. Grawoig. *Linear Programming: An Emphasis on Decision Making.* Reading, Mass.: Addison-Wesley, 1968.

Huntsberger, D.V., et. al. *Statistical Reference for Management and Economics.* Rockleigh, N.J. Allyn & Bacon.

Kazmier, Leonard J. *Statistical Analysis for Business and Economics.* New York: McGraw-Hill, 1973.

Lazzaro, Victor, ed. *Systems and Procedures: A Handbook for Business and Industry.* 2d ed. Englewood Cliffs, N.J.: Prentice-Hall, 1968.

Martin, F.F. *Bayesian Decision Problems and Markov Chains.* 1967. Reprint. Huntington, N.Y.: Robert E. Krieger Publishing Co., 1975.

Parsons, Robert. *Statistical Analysis: A Decision Making Approach.* New York: Harper & Row, 1974.

Schlaifer, Robert. *Analysis of Decisions Under Uncertainty.* New York: McGraw-Hill, 1969.

378 Fund Accounting

Henke, Emerson O. *Accounting for Nonprofit Organizations.* Belmont, Calif.: Wadsworth, 1966.

Kerrigan, Harry D. *Fund Accounting.* New York: McGraw-Hill 1969.

Lynn, Edward S., and Robert J. Freeman. *Fund Accounting.* Englewood Cliffs, N.J.: Prentice-Hall, 1974.

Mikesell, R.M., and Leon E. Hay. *Governmental Accounting.* 5th ed. Homewood, Ill.: Richard D. Irwin, 1974.

National Committee on Governmental Accounting. *Governmental Accounting, Auditing, and Financial Reporting.* Chicago: Municipal Finance Officers Association of the United States and Canada, 1968.

380 ORDERING PUBLICATIONS

The journals and other publications mentioned throughout this chapter are generally available from their respective publishers. AAA publications may be ordered directly from:
    American Accounting Association
    Paul L. Gerhardt, Administrative Secretary
    653 South Orange Avenue
    Sarasota, Florida 33577
AICPA publications may be obtained with an order form (see Exhibit 5-4) or by writing:
    American Institute of Certified Public Accountants
    1211 Avenue of the Americas
    New York, New York 10036

4
Accounting Associations and Regulatory Agencies

410 ACCOUNTING ASSOCIATIONS

This section contains a nonexhaustive list of accounting associations having a broad base of interest.

411 American Accounting Association (AAA),

653 Orange Avenue, Sarasota, Florida 33577

Founded 1916. This is an organization made up of educators and practitioners of accounting concerned with promoting education and research in accounting. Publications: (1) *Accounting Review,* quarterly; (2) Various special studies as the need dictates.

412 American Association of Attorney-Certified Public Accountants,

3225 S. Norwood, Tulsa, Oklahoma 74135

Founded 1964. Membership consists of persons who are licensed as both certified public accountants and as attorneys. This association is concerned with the professional and legal rights of those who are licensed to practice in the two professions. Publication: *Attorney-CPA,* quarterly.

413 American Institute of Certified Public Accountants (AICPA),

1211 Avenue of the Americas, New York, New York 10036.

Founded 1887. Membership consists of those persons certified to practice public accountancy by the states and territories of the United States. The AICPA is concerned with the continued development of the accounting profession in the changing business environment. Publications: (1) *CPA Letter,* semimonthly, (2) *Journal of Accountancy,* monthly; (3) *Tax Advisor* monthly; (4) *Management Advisor,* bimonthly.

414 American Society of Women Accountants (ASWA),

Suite 1036, 35 E. Wacker Drive, Chicago, Illinois 60601

Founded 1938. Membership consists of women in accounting education and practicing the profession of accounting. Publication: *The Woman C.P.A.,* quarterly.

415 American Woman's Society of Certified Public Accountants (AWSCPA),

P.O. Box 389, Marysville, Ohio 43040

Founded 1933. Membership consists of women who have passed the CPA exam and who may or may not have received the certifitcate. Other women meeting certain requirements may be associate members. This association is concerned with promoting women in the field of accounting. Publication: *The Woman CPA,* quarterly.

416 Federal Government Accountants Association (FGAA),

727 S. 23rd Street, Suite 120, Arlington, Virginia 22202.

Founded 1950. This is a professional organization of accountants, auditors, comptrollers, and budget officers employed by the various agencies of the federal government. Publications: (1) *Federal Financial Management Topics,* monthly; (2) *Federal Accountant,* quarterly.

417 National Association of Accountants (NAA),

919 Third Avenue, New York, New York 10022.

Founded 1919. Membership consists of accountants in public accounting, industry, government, and teaching as well as others who are interested in accounting matters. Publication: *Management Accounting,* monthly.

418 National Association of State Boards of Accountancy (NASBA),

666 Fifth Avenue, New York New York 10019.

Founded 1908. The membership of this asociation consists of members of the state boards of accounting and members of the Board of examiners of AICPA. The purpose is to promote uniform standards in all areas of accounting. Publications: (1) *News,* monthly: (2) *Annual Reports.*

419 National Society of Public Accountants (NSPA),

1717 Penn Avenue, N.W., Suite 1200, Washington, D.C. 20006.

Founded 1945. This group is concerned with the education of accountants. Publications: (1) *National Public Accountant,* monthly; (2) *NSPA Wasington Reporter,* monthly; (3) *Annual Report* (4) *Yearbook.*

420 THE FINANCIAL ACCOUNTING STANDARDS BOARD

The Financial Accounting Foundation, the Financial Accounting Standards Board, and the Financial Accounting Standards Advisory Council were established on June 30, 1972. The Financial Accounting Foundation is an independent body within the private sector. Its mission is to develop and issue standards of financial accounting and reporting for industrial and commercial corporations, partnerships, proprietorships, institutions, not-for-profit organizations, and other entities.[1]

The Financial Accounting Foundation is governed by a Board of Trustees made up of nine members. The duties of the Board of Trustees include:

1. To appoint the members of the Financial Accounting Standards Board.
2. To appoint the members of the Financial Accounting Standards Advisory Council.
3. To review periodically the basic structure of the standards-setting function, including by-laws of the Financial Accounting Foundation.

The Financial Accounting Standards Board (FASB) is made up of seven members appointed by the Board of Trustees. The seven members are full-time employees. Four of the members are CPAs drawn from the public practice; the other three members are to be competent in financial rreporting, whether certified or not. The FASB is responsible for issuing statements on financial accounting standards, including interpretation of those standards. The FASB is charged with acting independently of the Board of Trustees.

The Financial Accounting Standards Advisory Council members are appointed by the Board of Trustees. The Advisory Council is made up of individuals who are knowledgeable about the problems of financial reporting. No individual professional organizations or discipline may have predominant influence on the Advisory Council.

430 THE SECURITIES AND EXCHANGE COMMISSION

The general objective of the statutes administered by the Securities and Exchange Commission (SEC) is to provide the fullest possible disclosure to the investing public and to protect the interest of the public and investors against malpractices in the securities and financial markets. The SEC was created under authority of the Security Exchange Act of 1934 (48 Stat. 881: 15 U.S.C. 78a to 78jj), and was organized on July 2, 1934.[2] The SEC ruling body consists of a chairman plus four commissioners.

Some of the duties of the SEC include:

1. The Securities Act of 1933 requires issuers of securities making public offerings of securities in interstate commerce or througfh the mails, directly or by others on their behalf, to file with the Commission registration statements containing financial and other pertinent data about the issuer and the securities being offered. (p.567)

---

1. Committee on Rules of Procedure, Financial Accounting Foundation, "Financial Accounting Standards Board Proposed Rules of Procedure," *Journal of Accountancy*, (November 1972), pp. 75-78.

2. General Service Administration, Office of the Federal National Archives and Records Services, *U.S. Government Manual 1975-1976* (Washington, D.C.: U.S. Government Printing Office, 1975), p. 567.

2. The Securities Exchange Act of 1934 requires all national securities exchanges and national securities associations to register with the Commission and to adopt rules which are designed, among other things, to promote just and equitable principles of trade. (p. 569)
3. The Securities Exchange Act also requires the filing of registration applications and annual and other reports with national securities exchanges and the Commission by companies whose securities are listed upon the exchanges, by companies which have assets of $1 million or more and 500 or more shareholders of record, and by companies which distributed securities pursuant to a registration statement declared effective by the Commission under the Securities Act of 1933. (p. 569)
4. Brokers and dealers who engage in any over-the-counter securities business must register with the Commission. In addition, the Commission has broad rulemaking authority with respect to, among other things, short sales. (p. 569)
5. The Investment Company Act of 1940 provides for the registration with the Commission of investment companies and subjects their activities to regulation to protect investors. The regulation covers sales and management fees, composition of boards of directors and capital structure. (p. 570)
6. The PublicUtility Holding Company Act of 1935 provides for regulation by the Commission of the purchase and sale of securities and assets by companies in electric and gas utility holding company systems, their intrasystem transactions and service and management arrangements.[3] (p. 570)

3. Ibid., pp. 567-70.

5
Accounting Education

510 ADVANCED DEGREES

The advanced degrees often held by accountants include Ph.D (doctor of philosophy), D.B.A. (doctor of busines administration), M.B.A. (master of business administration), and M.S. (master of science), with major fields in accounting.

511 Master's Programs

The AICPA staff surveyed 485 colleges in early 1976 as to the projected supply of accounting graduates in the United States for the academic year 1975-76 and their predictions for the next five years.[1] Based on a return of about 71 percent of the colleges surveyed, the projections shown in Exhibit 5-1 were made.

Exhibit 5-1
Projected Supply of Graduates with Master's Degrees in Accounting

School Year	Number
1976-77	6,100
1977-78	6,900
1978-79	7,800
1979-80	8,400

Source: Daniel L. Sweeney, *The Supply of Accounting Graduates and the Demand for Public Accounting Recruits* (New York: AICPA, Spring 1976), p. 7

There is a difference in the entry pay of persons holding bachelor's degrees and those holding master's degrees. In government, the master's degree may qualify a person for a GS-7 rather than a GS-5 for the bachelor's degree, an increase in entry pay of over $2,000 annually. This may also be true in public accounting and industry depending on the specialized need of the potential employer.

---

1. Daniel L. Sweeney, *The Supply of Accounting Graduates and the Demand for Public Accounting Recruits* (New York: AICPA, Spring 1976), p. 2.

512 Doctoral Programs

The demand for accounting professors with doctor's degrees continues to exceed the projected supply. The American Accounting Association's paper "Report on Supply and Demand for Accounting Professors" contained information collected in a questionnaire sent to over 500 colleges and universities throughout the United States.[2] The questionnaire was designed to collect information concerning the number of accounting students in the course work stage and in the dissertation stage, and the number of full-time accounting faculty members which college and universities expect to hire in 1977-1978, 1978-1979, and 1979-1980. Information concerning the number of candidates are presented in Exhibit 5-2.

Exhibit 5-2
Expected Supply of Doctoral Candidates

	Total	Male	Female
1. Number of doctoral candidates in residence			
a. in course work stage	490	395	95
b. in dissertation stage	163	142	21
Total	653	537	116
2. Number of doctoral candidates not in residence			
a. in course work stage	53	42	11
b. in dissertation stage	183	165	18
	236	207	29
3. Number who expect to seek full-time positions	Between Oct. 1, 1976 and Sept. 30, 1977	Starting After Oct. 1, 1977	
a. Male	133	138	
b. Female	29	29	
Total	162	167	

The schools surveyed were asked how many full-time accounting faculty members they were authorized to hire for the 1977-78 academic year., The responses of the 260 of the 500 colleges and universities surveyed responding to this and related questions are presented in Exhibit 5-3.

The demand for Ph.D's has been greater than the supply for some time and is expected to continue for the next few years. Looking at the demand side of the market for accounting Ph.D. students in the 1974-75 academic year, Professor Willard E. Stone found that Professor Crum's fear of a shortage of accounting educators is currently well founded. In a 1974-75 study of 14 universities with large accounting departments, an average shortage of 3.5 Ph.D. holders per university was indicated.[3]

2. Paul L. Gerhardt, *1976-77 Report on Supply and Demand for Accounting Professors* (Sarasota, Florida.: American Accounting Association, January 1977).
3. Williard E. Stone, "The Accounting Ph.D. Marketplace—Updated 1974-75," *Journal of Accountancy*, (October 1974), p. 104.

Exhibit 5-3
Accounting Faculty Demand

a.	Demand and degree requirement:	
	1. 1977-78 academic year	
	a. hold a Ph.D. or D.B.A.	311
	b. be at the doctoral dissertation stage	146
	c. be at the doctoral course stage	12
	d. hold a Masters/CPA, or JD/CPA	94
	e. hold a Masters or JD, but *not* CPA	15
	Total	578
	2. 1978-79 academic year, total	378
	3. 1979-80 academic year, total	351

The continued shortage of accounting professors holding doctorates may well continue for the next decade. The increased demand for more highly trained professionals in accounting by the public and private sectors as well as in government funnels many potential teachers away from eduction.

520 AMERICAN ACCOUNTING ASSOCIATION PROGRAMS

Much of the work of the AAA is carried on through committees. During 1974-75, there were twenty-six major committees and several subcommittees and task forces in operation. Some of the committees and task forces completed their projects and published reports. Those reports included the following:

1. *Report of the Committee on Professional Examinations.* This committee was charged with informing educators of the nature and content of examinations, experience, and educational requirements in certification programs that test accounting knowledge; more specifically, the CPA, CMA, and CIA examination material was reviewed and evaluated.[4]
2. *Report of the Committee on Accounting for Social Purposes.* This committee was charged with reviewing current effort in accounting for corporate social performance.[5]
3. *Reports to the FASB from the Price-Level Reporting Subcommittee, April 1974.* The principal conclusion reached by members of this subcommittee was that reporting the efforts of price changes or price-level changes should be required.[6] The committee members did not agree on how this should be done.

---

4. "Report of the Committee on Professional Examinations," *Accounting Review*, supplement to vol XLXI (1976), p.3.
5. "Report of the Committee on Accounting for Social Performance," *Accounting Review*, supplement to vol. XLXI (1976), p. 41.
6. "Reports to the FASB from the Price-Level Reporting Committee," *Accounting Review*, supplement to vol. XLXI (1976), p. 215.

There are many committees working on various asignments. Some have reported their findings and recommendations; others are still doing research and reviewing data relative to their projects. Some of those committees include:

1. A committee to Prepare a Statement of Objectives for the American Accounting Association.
2. A standing committee on Concepts and Standards—External Financial Reports.
3. A standing committee on Concepts and Standards—Management Planning and Control.
4. A Committee on Accounting in the Public Sector.

The programs of the American Accounting Association reflect the problems that professionals are currently facing in their day-to-day operations. They also include programs to anticipate the challenges of the future as well as those current or continuing problems for which an acceptable solution has not yet been determined.

530 PROFESSIONAL DEVELOPMENT AICPA

The continued professional development of its members is of prime concern to the AICPA. A large share of its budget is expended in research and studies of means to recruit candidates into the profession who have the proper training and background for entry-level positions. The AICPA distributes material for use in obtaining the body of knowledge necessary to fulfill the demands placed on the public accountants by the users of their service.

The catalog, *AICPA Publications and Self-Study Materials,* 1977, is typical of the effort of AICPA in distributing information to its members. This catalog lists all publications, subscriptions services, recorded material and self-study programs available from the AICPA as of May 1, 1977. Discounts of 20 percent are available to members of the AICPA and of 40 percent off list price to schools and teachers. In addition, there are also quantity discounts. An AICPA order form is shown in Exhibit 5-4.

Professional development is a joint responsibility of the individual, the profession (represented by AAA, AICPA, NAA, and other professional organizations), the many CPA firms, and accountants in industry and government. The development of a profession involves a balance between initial academic preparation and on-the-job experience with progressively more challenging work situations, interspersed with formal training programs. The rapid pace of change in EDP technology, tax law pronouncements, and the more exacting requirements of the SEC and other regulatory bodies all require that the professional's body of knowledge be continually updated. The individual has many sources of help in maintaining a pattern of growth in the profession of accounting.

Accounting Education   113

**Exhibit 5-4
AICPA Publications Order Form**

Publications Order Form

Publications are listed by subject category in the same order in which they appear in the catalog. The page references at the left of each column can also help you locate specific titles. Magazines and other subscription services are listed separately on page 68.

All domestic orders will be shipped postpaid. *Before returning the form, be sure to total your order and fill out your name and address on page 68.*

CPE self-study materials should be ordered by means of the separate form which starts on page 69.

3 ☐ Accounting Trends & Techniques (009768) 30.00

4 Technical Practice Aids
(see subscription services, page 68)
SEC Quarterly
(see CPE subscription services, page 71)

5 AICPA Professional Standards
(see subscription services, page 68)

6 GAAP for Smaller and/or Closely Held Businesses (056006) 2.00
AICPA Professional Standards Paperback
(available to AICPA members only)
☐ Vol. 1: Auditing, MAS, Tax Practice (003615) .... no discount 4.50
☐ Vol. 2: Ethics, Bylaws, Quality Control (003620) .... no discount 4.00
☐ Vol. 3: Accounting-Current Text (003634) .... no discount 8.00
☐ 3 Volume Set (003600) no discount 13.50
☐ Accounting—Original Pronouncements (003649) .... no discount 8.00

7 ☐ Corporate Financial Reporting: The Benefits and Problems of Disclosure (024927) .... no discount 12.00

8 Accounting Research Monographs
☐ 1: Accounting for Depreciable Assets (042003) 6.00
☐ 2: Market Value Methods for Intercorporate Investments in Stock (042018) 5.50

8 Industry Accounting Guides
☐ Franchise Fee Revenue (062007) 2.75
☐ Retail Land Sales (062011) 2.75
☐ Profit Recognition on Sales of Real Estate (062026) 2.75
☐ Motion Picture Films (062030) 2.75

9 Financial Report Surveys
☐ 1: Accounting Policy Disclosure (037607) 4.50
☐ 2: Reporting Accounting Changes (037611) 5.50
☐ 3: Reporting the Results of Operations (037626) 6.50
☐ 4: Interperiod Tax Allocation (037630) 7.00
☐ 5: Statement of Changes in Financial Position (037645) 6.50
☐ 6: Summary of Operations and Related Management Discussion and Analysis (037650) 8.50
☐ 7: Departures From the Auditor's Standard Report (037664) 7.50
☐ 8: Disclosure of Related Party Transactions (037679) 6.00

☐ 9: Disclosure of Subsequent Events (037683) 7.00
☐ 10: Accounting for Contingencies (037698) 7.50
☐ 11: Disclosure of "Pro Forma" Calculations (037700) 7.50
☐ 12: Accounting for Marketable Equity Securities (037715) 7.50

10 Objectives of Financial Statements—
☐ Report (025309) 4.50
☐ Papers (025313) 14.00
☐ Computing Earnings Per Share (028504) 5.00
☐ Accounting for Income Taxes (003507) 4.00

11 Accounting Research Studies
☐ 1: Basic Postulates of Accounting (008106) 4.00
☐ 2: "Cash Flow" Analysis & the Funds Statement (008200) 5.00
☐ 3: Broad Accounting Principles (008303) 4.00
☐ 4: Reporting Leases in Financial Statements (008407) 5.00
☐ 5: Accounting for Business Combinations (008500) 5.00
☐ 6: Financial Effects of Price-Level Changes (008604) 6.00
☐ 7: Inventory of GAAP (008712) 8.00
☐ 8: Accounting for Cost of Pension Plans (008801) 5.50
☐ 9: Allocation of Corporate Income Taxes (008905) 5.00
☐ 10: Accounting for Goodwill (009005) 5.50
☐ 11: Reporting in Extractive Industries (009109) 5.50
☐ 12: Foreign Operations in U.S. Dollars (009202) 5.00
☐ 13: Accounting Basis of Inventories (009306) 6.00
☐ 14: Accounting for R&D Expenditures (009400) 5.50
☐ 15: Stockholder's Equity (009503) 8.50
☐ Post Binder (008002) 7.00
☐ Statement of Issues: Scope and Organization of the Study of Auditor's Responsibilities (010553) 1.75

12 ☐ APB Opinions Nos. _____ each 1.00
☐ Post Binder (038008) 7.00
APB Statements
☐ 3: Financial Statements Restated for General Pricing Level Changes (058035) 3.00
☐ 4: Basic Concepts & Accounting Principles (058040) 3.50

13 ☐ Federal Financial Management: Accounting and Auditing Practices (034007) 14.00
APB Opinion Series
(see CPE order form, page 69)

continued on next page . . .

Note: Reprinted by permission of the publisher from *AICPA Publications and Self-Study Materials* (New York: AICPA, 1977), pp. 65-71. Copyright © 1977 by the American Institute of Certified Public Accountants, Inc.

Exhibit 5-4 (continued)

Publications Order Form

14 Accountants International Studies
- 1: Accounting & Auditing Approaches to Inventories (002010) ... 3.50
- 2: Independent Auditor's Reporting Standards (002025) ... 3.50
- 3: Using the Work and Report of Another Auditor (002030) ... 3.50
- 4: Accounting for Corporate Income Taxes (002044) ... 3.50
- 5: Reporting by Diversified Cos. (002059) ... 3.50
- 6: Consolidated Financial Statements (002063) ... 3.50
- 7: The Funds Statement (002078) ... 3.50
- 8: Materiality in Accounting (002082) ... 3.50
- 9: Extraordinary Items, Prior Period Adjustments, Changes in Accounting Principles (002097) ... 3.50
- 10: Published Profit Forecasts (002100) ... 3.50
- 11: International Financial Reporting (002114) ... 3.50
- 12: Glossary of Accounting Terms (002129) ... 3.50
- 13: Accounting for Goodwill (002133) ... 3.50
- 14: Interim Financial Reporting (002148) ... 3.50
- 15: Going Concern Problems (002152) ... 3.50
- 16: Independence of Auditors (002167) ... 3.50
- 17: Audit Committees (002171) ... 3.50
- 18: Accounting for Pension Costs (002186) ... 3.50
- Post Binder (002006) ... 7.00

14 Statements on International Accounting Standards
- Preface; No. 1: Disclosure of Accounting Policies (036002) ... 2.50
- 2: Valuation and Presentation of Inventories (036017) ... 2.00
- 3: Consolidated Financial Statements (036021) ... 2.00
- 4: Depreciation Accounting (036036) ... 2.00
- 5: Information to be Disclosed in Financial Statements (036040) ... 2.00

15
- Professional Accounting in 30 Countries (010002) ... 35.00
- Suggested Guidelines for Audit Guides Prepared by Federal Agencies (059803) ... 2.00
- Auditing Standards Established by GAO (013335) ... 2.00

16
- Auditor's Study and Evaluation of Internal Control in EDP Systems (013602) ... 4.50

Auditing Research Monographs
- 1: The Auditor's Reporting Obligation (020019) ... 5.00
- 2: Behavior of Major Statistical Estimators (020023) ... 8.50

17 Statements on Auditing Standards
- Codification of SAS Nos. 1 to 15 (058548) ... 6.00
- SAS Statements No. _____ each 1.25
- Post Binder (058764) ... 7.00
- Auditing and EDP (013509) ... 14.00

18 Auditor's Approach to Statistical Sampling
(see CPE order form, page 69)
- Computer Control Guidelines (024109) ... 12.50
- Computer Audit Guidelines (024005) ... 23.50
- Combination of Above (024202) ... 31.25

19 Industry Audit Guides
- Guide for Engagement of CPAs to Prepare Unaudited Financial Statements (013373) ... 3.50
- Government Contractors (013369) ... 4.50
- Service-Center-Produced Records (013354) ... 4.50
- State and Local Governmental Units (013340) ... 6.00
- Voluntary Health & Welfare Organizations (012120) ... 4.50
- Investment Companies (012116) ... 6.00
- Finance Companies (013316) ... 5.00
- Colleges and Universities (013320) ... 5.00
- Stock Life Insurance Cos. (013301) ... 6.00
- Savings & Loan Assns. (012510) ... 5.00
- Brokers and Dealers in Securities (012012) ... 6.00
- Hospital Audit Guide (012402) ... 4.00
- Employee Health & Welfare Benefit Funds (012309) ... 4.00
- Medicare Audit Guide (012205) ... 4.00
- Banks (011128) ... 5.00
- Personal Financial Statements (013104) ... 3.50
- Fire and Casualty Insurance Cos. (011908) ... 5.00
- Construction Contractors (010604) ... 5.00
- Post Binder (011005) ... 7.00

20 CPA Client Bulletin
(see subscription services, page 68)
Sample Engagement Letters for an Accounting Practice
(see CPE order form, page 69)

21 ☐ MAP Handbook (042624) 3 vol. 120.00

22 Secretarial Orientation to Public Accounting (see CPE order form, page 69)

23 The Tax Adviser
(see subscription services, page 68)

24 ☐ Working With the Revenue Code—1977 (075774) ... 10.00
Tax Principles to Remember
(see CPE order form, page 69)

25 ☐ Tax Research Techniques (059254) ... 18.50

26 ☐ Tax Practice Management (059240) ... 38.50

Tax Highlights Quarterly
(see CPE subscription services, page 71)

27 ☐ Codification of Statements on Responsibilities in Tax Practice (068003) ... 2.50

Statements of Tax Policy
- 1: Taxation of Capital Gains (058110) ... 2.50
- 2: Value-Added Tax (058124) ... 3.00
- 3: Elimination of the Double Tax on Dividends (058139) ... 3.00
- 4: Estate & Gift Tax Reform (058143) ... 3.00

28 Management Education Portfolio
(see CPE order form, page 69)

29 MAS Special Reports
- Energy Conservation Studies (048508) ... 2.50
- Environmental Cost/Benefit Studies (048512) ... 2.50
- MAS by CPAs—Study of Required Knowledge (058872) ... 8.00
- Statements on MAS (058849) ... 2.50

continued on next page ...

Exhibit 5-4 (continued)

30 MAS Guidelines Series
- ☐ 1: Administration of the MAS Practice (045110) ... 3.50
- ☐ 2: Documentation for MAS Engagements (045124) ... 5.50
- ☐ 3: Guidelines for Systems for the Preparation of Financial Forecasts (046004) ... 3.00
- ☐ 4: Guidelines for Development and Implementation of Computer-Based Application Systems (047011) ... 3.50
- ☐ 5: Guidelines for Cooperative MAS Engagement (047026) ... 2.50

31
- ☐ 6: Guidelines for CPA Participation in Government Audit Engagements to Evaluate Economy, Efficiency, and Program Results (047030) ... 5.00
- ☐ 7: Interpretations of MAS Practice Standards (047045) ... 2.50
- ☐ Statement of Position on Presentation and Disclosure of Financial Forecasts (058904) ... 2.00

MAS Technical Studies
- ☐ 1: Analysis for Product Line Decisions (069100) ... 4.50
- ☐ 2: Analysis for Pricing & Distribution Policies (069203) ... 4.50
- ☐ 3: Analysis for Expansion or Contraction of a Business (069307) ... 4.50
- ☐ 4: Analysis for Purchasing and Financing Productive Equipment (069400) ... 4.50
- ☐ 5: Analysis for Purchase or Sale of a Business (069504) ... 4.50
- ☐ 6: Practical Techniques and Policies for Inventory Control (069608) ... 4.50
- ☐ 7: Techniques for Product Forecasting (069701) ... 4.50
- ☐ 8: Management Information Systems for the Smaller Business (069805) ... 4.50
- ☐ 9: Production Scheduling (069909) ... 4.50
- ☐ Post Binder (069006) ... 7.00

32 FAIM Reference Services
(available to AICPA members only)

FAIM Management Service
- ☐ EDP Review (091000) no discount ... 850.00
- ☐ EDP Management (091014) no discount ... 420.00
- ☐ Security (091029) no discount ... 245.00
- ☐ Software Packages (091033) no discount ... 420.00
- ☐ Complete Set (091048) no discount ... 1,825.00

FAIM Technical Service
- ☐ Security Evaluator (091052) no discount ... 80.00
- ☐ Systems Performance Measurement (091067) no discount ... 80.00
- ☐ Front End Evaluator (091071) no discount ... 80.00
- ☐ EDP Applications Improvement (091086) no discount ... 165.00
- ☐ Complete Set (091090) no discount ... 385.00
- ☐ Entire Management and Technical Reference Series (091103) no discount ... 2,100.00

33 Computer Services Guidelines
- ☐ 1: General Systems Specifications for a Computer System (047007) ... 4.00

- ☐ 2: Guidelines To Assess Computerized Tax Return Systems (047505) ... 3.00
- ☐ Ring Binder for Computer Services Guidelines (046907) ... 8.00
- ☐ Computer Systems Exchange (022508) ... 10.00 (Available to AICPA members in public practice only)

34 DATAPRO Subscription Services
(see subscription services, page 68)

35 AUERBACH Data Processing Management
(see subscription services, page 68)

36 Accounting Articles Digest
(see CPE subscription services, page 71)
- ☐ Businessmen's Information Guide (012600) ... 3.50
- ☐ Businessmen's Information Guide—Spanish Ed. (012703) ... 3.50
- ☐ Social Measurement (311008) ... 6.00

37
- ☐ Measurement of Corporate Social Performance (025205) ... 10.00
- ☐ Lawyers & CPAs: A Study of Interprofessional Relations (042501) ... 2.50

38
- ☐ Getting Started in the CPA Profession (882309) 16 mm film ... 100.00

39 Accountants' Index
- ☐ 1976 (000250) ... 42.50
- ☐ 1975 (000246) ... 42.50
- ☐ 1974 (000231) ... 42.50
- ☐ 1973 (000227) ... 42.50
- ☐ 1972 (000212) ... 35.00
- ☐ 1971 (000208) ... 35.00

Accountants' Index Quarterly Subscription Service
(see subscription services, page 68)

Accountancy Law Reports
(see subscription services, page 68)

40
- ☐ Code of Professional Ethics (881755) ... 2.50

Rise of the Accounting Profession
- ☐ Vol. 1 (051017) ... 12.50
- ☐ Vol. II (051021) ... 15.00
- ☐ Compliance with Federal Election Campaign Requirements (305007) ... 16.50
- ☐ Campaign Treasurer's Handbook (304004) ... 3.00

41 THE CPA Letter
(see subscription services, page 68)
- ☐ Managing Public School Dollars (311101) ... 2.00

42
- ☐ How to Choose and Use a CPA (337703) (minimum order 10 copies) ... .25
- ☐ You and the Profession (889204) (minimum order 10 copies) ... .25
- ☐ What Does a CPA Do? (337506) (minimum order 10 copies) ... .25
- ☐ Going Public (314006) (minimum order 10 copies) ... .35

43 AICPA Washington Report
(see subscription services, page 68)
- ☐ New Guides to Better Accounting (054119) ... 4.00

44
- ☐ CPA Exam Supplement (latest date) ... 2.00

CPA Examination Official Questions
- ☐ 1974-1975 (071203) ... 4.50
- ☐ 1972-1973 (071100) ... 4.50
- ☐ 1969-1971 (071006) ... 5.50

continued on next page ...

Exhibit 5-4 (continued)

Publications Order Form — PAGE 68

CPA Examination Unofficial Answers	
☐ 1974-1975 (073209)	4.50
☐ 1972-1973 (073105)	4.50
☐ 1969-1971 (073001)	6.50

45 The Journal of Accountancy
(see subscription services, page 68)

Magazine Binders
☐ Journal of Accountancy (400023) 7.00
☐ Tax Adviser (200021) 7.00

46 ☐ Schools of Accountancy: A Look at the Issues (052202) 3.00

47 Executive Checklist for Finance and Administration
Add 'n' Stac Modules
Muradapter
(see CPE order form, page 69)

48 CPAudio Numbered Series
(see CPE order form, page 69)

Total order _____
Less 20% AICPA member discount _____
Net remittance enclosed _____

SUBSCRIPTION SERVICES

The Journal of Accountancy
☐ 1 year 15.00
☐ 3 years 36.00

With CPA Examinations
☐ 1 year 19.00
☐ 3 years 48.00

Accountants' Index
☐ 1 year 135.00
AICPA Members
☐ 1 year 108.00

The CPA Letter
☐ 1 year 25.00
(AICPA members receive The CPA Letter free of charge.)

The Tax Adviser
☐ 1 year 36.00
☐ 3 years 85.00
AICPA Members
☐ 1 year 28.00
☐ 3 years 68.00

Washington Report
☐ 1 year 38.00
AICPA Members
☐ 1 year 30.00

Accountancy Law Reports
☐ 1 year 85.00
Not subject to AICPA member discount.

AVAILABLE TO AICPA MEMBERS ONLY

AICPA Professional Standards
Subscriptions through May 31, 1978
☐ Vol. 1 .... 44.00
☐ Vol. 2 .... 44.00
☐ Vol. 3 .... 52.00
☐ Three services in combination 104.00

Technical Practice Aids
☐ Through May 31, 1978 .... 34.00
☐ 4 Volumes (including 3-volume Professional Standards services) 126.00

CPA Client Bulletin
50 monthly copies (minimum order)
3 months $30.00   1 year $100.00
Additional lots of 25 available at $7.50 per quarter or $25.00 per-year.
_____ quantity ordered.
☐ 3 months   ☐ 1 year

☐ AUERBACH Data Processing Management 1 year 140.00

FOR AICPA MEMBERS IN PUBLIC PRACTICE ONLY

☐ DATAPRO 70 1 year 190.00
☐ DATAPRO 70 with Telephone Consulting Service 1 year 270.00
☐ DATAPRO Reports on Minicomputers 1 year 175.00

☐ DATAPRO Reports on Office Systems 1 year 175.00
☐ DATAPRO Directory of Software 1 year 170.00

10151

---

name _____

firm (if part of mailing address) _____

address _____

city _____ state _____ zip _____

Except in the case of subscription services, please add 8% sales tax in New York City. Elsewhere in New York State add 4% State tax plus local tax if applicable.

continued on next page . . .

Exhibit 5-4 (continued)

CPE Self-Study Materials Order Form

CPE self-study materials are listed by subject category in the same order in which they appear in the catalog. The page references at the left of each column can also help you locate specific titles. CPE subscription services are listed separately on page 71.

All domestic orders will be shipped postpaid. *Before returning the form, be sure to total your order and fill out your name and address on page 71.*

Publications should be ordered by means of the separate form which starts on page 65.

PAGE

13 ☐ APB Opinion Series No. _____ each 10.00

18 **Auditor's Approach to Statistical Sampling**
☐ Vol. 1: Introduction to Statistical Concepts and Estimation of Dollar Values (724016) 10.00
☐ Vol. 2: Sampling for Attributes: Estimation and Discovery (724020) ... 10.00
☐ Vol. 3: Stratified Random Sampling (724035) 10.00
☐ Vol. 5: Ratio and Difference Estimation (724054) 10.00
☐ Vol. 6: Field Manual (724069) 10.00
☐ Post Binder for Series (724001) 7.00

20 ☐ Sample Engagement Letters for an Accounting Practice (723973) 15.00

22 ☐ Secretarial Orientation to Public Accounting (723935) 15.00

24 ☐ Tax Principles to Remember (723969) 28.50

26 **Tax Highlights Quarterly**
(see subscription services, page 71)

28 **Management Education Portfolio**
(see description for quantity discounts.)
Management and the Computer
☐ Computer Basics for Management (720015) 50.00
☐ The EDP Feasibility Study (720020) .. 50.00
☐ Managing the Human Element in EDP (720034) 50.00
☐ Management Information Systems (720049) 50.00
☐ Quantitative Aids to Decision Making (720053) 50.00
☐ Basic Systems and Procedures (720410) 50.00

Marketing Management
☐ Modern Marketing and Company Objectives (720119) 50.00
☐ The Management of Personal Selling (720138) 50.00
☐ Advertising: Strategy and Design (720123) 50.00
☐ Strategies in Marketing Research (720142) 50.00
☐ Marketing and the Computer (720157) 50.00

☐ How to be a Successful Product Manager (720617) 50.00

Managerial Finance and Control
☐ Macroeconomics and Company Planning (720212) 50.00
☐ The Theory and Practice of Management Control (720250) 50.00
☐ Planning Cash Flow (720227) 50.00
☐ Capital Structure and Long-Term Objectives (720231) 50.00
☐ Return On Investment (720424) 50.00
☐ Commercial Banking (720509) 50.00
☐ Managing Corporate Cash (720551) .. 50.00
☐ Performing the Operations Audit (720392) 50.00
☐ Managing Credit for Profit (720443) .. 50.00
☐ Planning and Administering the Company Budget (720373) 50.00
☐ Budgeting by Department and Functional Area (720388) 50.00
☐ Accounting For Managers (720246) .. 50.00
☐ Basics of Cost Accounting (720405) . 50.00

General Management Skills
☐ Communication Skills for Managers (720566) 50.00
☐ Training and Developing Today's Work Force (720335) 50.00
☐ What Managers Do (720316) 50.00
☐ A Manager's Guide to Human Behavior (720570) 50.00
☐ Transactional Analysis for Managers (720585) 50.00
☐ Getting Results with Time Management (720528) 50.00
☐ Planning and Control for Managers (720439) 50.00
☐ The Executive Guide to Wage and Salary Administration (720513) 50.00
☐ Personal Financial Planning (720590) 50.00
☐ Management Strategies for the Small Firm (720602) 50.00

47 Executive Checklist. Finance & Administration (740201) 130.00
Add 'N' Stac Modules
☐ Brown (723282) 1.70
☐ Black (723278) 1.70
☐ Muradapter (723297) 45.00

48 **CPAudio Numbered Series**
☐ Nos. 37-52 .... 10.00
☐ Nos. 7-36 .... 8.00

continued on next page...

Exhibit 5-4 (continued)

CPE Self-Study Materials Order Form *PAGE 70*

PAGE		
49	☐ Reporting on Unaudited Financial Statements (715360)	30.00
	___Additional Workbooks (715375)*	___
50	☐ General Standards (715411)	30.00
	___Additional Workbooks (715426)*	___
	☐ Standards of Reporting and the Auditor's Standard Report (715430)	35.00
	___Additional Workbooks (715445)*	___
	☐ Standards of Field Work (715450)	43.00
	___Additional Workbooks (715464)*	___
51	☐ Statement of Changes in Financial Position (715303)	30.00
	___Additional Workbooks (715318)*	___
	☐ LIFO Inventory Accounting (712131)	15.00
	☐ Retail Audit Training (715520)	50.00
	___Additional Workbooks (715534) 1-20 $15; 21-50 $13; over 50 $10	___
52	**Industry Audit Guide Series**	
	☐ Audits of Personal Financial Statements (714000)	20.00
	☐ Audits of State and Local Governmental Units (740127)	20.00
	☐ Audits of Colleges and Universities (740146)	20.00
53	☐ Tax Reform Act Of 1976 (713120)	20.00
	___Additional Workbooks (713134) @	3.00
	☐ Estate Planning Strategies under the 1976 Tax Reform Act (713168)	20.00
	___Additional Workbooks (713172) @	3.00
	☐ Tax Shelters and the 1976 Tax Reform Act (713149)	20.00
	___Additional Workbooks (713153) @	3.00
	☐ Fundamentals of Tax Research (723954)	15.00
54	☐ Practical Approach to Preparing Form 1040 (715623)	35.00
	___Additional Workbooks (715638)*	___
	☐ Advanced 1040 Problems (715657)	40.00
	___Additional Workbooks (715661)*	___
	☐ Practical Approach to Preparing Form 1120 (715380)	35.00
	___Additional Workbooks (715394)*	___
55	**Key Code Section Series**	
	☐ Section 351: How to Incorporate a Business (715676)	20.00
	☐ Section 302: Distributions of Redemption of Stock (715708)	20.00
	☐ Section 331 & 346: Tax Treatment of Shareholders in Complete and Partial Liquidations (715712)	20.00
	☐ Section 332: Complete Liquidations of Subsidiaries (715727)	20.00
56	☐ Problems of the Closely Held Corporation (715587)	40.00
	___Additional Workbooks (715591)*	___
	☐ Guide to Corporate Tax Planning (713045)	25.00
	___Additional Quizzers (713050)	3.00

	☐ N.Y. State Franchise Tax (715549)	32.00
	___Additional Workbooks (715553)	8.00
57	☐ Estate, Gift, Income Taxation and Planning for Estates and Trusts (710121)	125.00
	___Additional Study Manuals (710136) @ 1-20 $16 each; 21-50 $14 each; over 50 $11 each	___
	___Examinations (710140) @ 10.00	___
58	**Pension and Profit Sharing Series**	
	☐ Part I: Individual Retirement Accounts (713064)	25.00
	___Additional Workbooks (713079) @	3.00
	☐ Part II: Fundamentals of Pension and Profit-Sharing Plans (713083)	25.00
	___Additional Workbooks (713098) @	3.00
	Entire Pension and Profit Sharing Series (713100)	45.00
	Workbooks for Entire Series (713115)	6.00
	☐ Earnings and Profits/Accumulated Earnings Tax (715604)	40.00
	___Additional Workbooks (715619)*	___
59	☐ Ins and Outs of IRS Practice and Procedure (713007)	35.00
	___Additional Workbooks (713011) 1-9 $12; 10-49 $10.80; 50-99 $9.60; 100 and over $8.40	___
	☐ Subchapter S Corporations (715322)	45.00
	___Additional Workbooks (715337)*	___
	☐ Practical Approach to Insolvencies and Bankruptcies (712150)	20.00
60	☐ CPA's Professional Liability (740108)	25.00
	___Additional Workbooks (740112)*	___
	☐ Physicians & Dentists including Veterinarians (740080)	50.00
	___Additional Workbooks (740095) 1-9 $15; 10-49 $13.50; 50-99 $12.00; 100 and over $10.50	___
	☐ Professional Ethics for CPAs (723992)	15.00
61	☐ Executive Writing, Speaking and Listening Skills (720532)	85.00
	___Additional Workbooks (720547) 1-10 $9.00; 11-24 $8.10; 25-49 $7.65; 50-99 $7.38; 100 or more $7.20	___
	☐ How to Prepare Engagement Letters (715568)	32.00
	___Additional Workbooks (715572)	8.00
	☐ Operational Auditing (740038)	32.00
	___Additional Workbooks (740004)	8.00
62	☐ Practice Growth Through Effective Public Relations (723920)	27.00
	☐ Introduction to Local Government Accounting (740057)	85.00
	___Additional Workbooks (740061) 1-9 $15; 10-49 $13.50; 50-99 $12; 100 or more $10.50	___

Exhibit 5-4 (continued)

Basic Staff Training Program

☐ Accounts Receivable (715021)	55.00	
___Additional Workbooks (715036)*	___	
☐ Inventories (715040)	55.00	
___Additional Workbooks (715055)*	___	
☐ Cash (715060)	55.00	
___Additional Workbooks (715074)*	___	
☐ Shareholders Equity (715089)	50.00	
___Additional Workbooks (715093)*	___	
☐ Long Term Assets I (715106)	50.00	
___Additional Workbooks (715110)*	___	
☐ Long Term Assets II (715125)	50.00
___Additional Workbooks (715130)*	___
☐ Current Liabilities (715144)	50.00
___Additional Workbooks (715159)*	___
☐ Long Term & Other Liabilities (715163)	50.00
___Additional Workbooks (715178)*	___
☐ Internal Control (715182)	50.00
___Additional Workbooks (715197)*	___
☐ Flowcharting (715200)	50.00
___Additional Workbooks (715214)*	___

---

*Additional Workbooks

Note: The following prices for additional workbooks apply to programs marked with an asterisk(*). Workbook prices for other programs are shown in the price schedule. *These prices apply only to multiple orders for the same module.*

1-9 Additional Workbooks	each	$12.50
10-49 Additional Workbooks	each	11.25
50-99 Additional Workbooks	each	10.00
100 and over Additional Workbooks	each	8.75

Subscriptions Available from CPE Division

☐ Accounting Articles Digest   1 year 40.00   ☐ Tax Highlights Quarterly   1 year 35.00
☐ SEC Quarterly   1 year 35.00

Total remittance enclosed _____

10151

name
firm (if part of mailing address)
address
city   state   zip

Except in the case of subscription services, please add 8% sales tax in New York City. Elsewhere in New York State add 4% State tax plus local tax if applicable.

540 PROFESSIONAL SCHOOLS OF ACCOUNTANCY

The AICPA established a Board on Standards for Programs and Schools of Professional Accounting in July of 1974. The charge to the board was as follows:

> The Board is directed to identify those standards that, when satisfied by a school, would justify its recognition by the accounting profession. Particular attention should be given to the criteria for the school's curriculum which would be appropriate for a professional program of accounting.[7]

The AICPA Board on Standards for Programs and Schools of Professional Accounting had several observations. In regard to the profession and its educational needs, the Board observed that professional accounting includes:

1. Comprehension of the total system of financial information flow and its relation to other systems in generating, analyzing, and communicating data useful to management, the public, or governmental agencies.
2. Ability to present financial information in conformity with generally accepted accounting principles.
3. Ability to audit in accordance with generally accepted evaluation of the system used in developing the financial data and for presenting fairly the information in financial statements.[8]

The object of the professional educational program would be to graduate an entry-level professional accountant. The board maintained that

> such an objective cannot be achieved within the traditional baccalaureate program. An adequate professional education in accounting will require at least two years of professional education and no less than three years of professional accounting. However, consideration should also be given to professional programs at the postbaccalaureate level; at this level professionalization may be most feasible, and it is to this level that the educational programs of the traditional learned professions have evolved.[9]

There are problems associated with a five-year professional program. One problem could be that the potential employee would be held back from the market for an additional year. This could result in students ending their fourth year and, prior to taking many of the courses required for taking the CPA exam, being recruited by CPA firms.

This and other problems associated with the development of professional schools of accounting are being studied by the accounting profession.

---

7. Discussion draft, "Board on Standards for Programs and Schools of Professional Accounting," American Institute of Certified Public Accountants, 1976, p. 1.
8. Ibid., pp. 1-2.
9. Ibid., p. 2.

6
Sample Corporation Annual Report

There are two basic types of financial reports prepared by businesses: (1) those prepared for use by managers for decision-making purposes, and (2) those prepared for outside or external users. External users include present owners, prospective investors, financial institutions, and employees.

Financial reports prepared for external users include the following:

1. *Annual reports to stockholders* (a sample financial statement is included in this section).
2. *Tax returns* including (1) federal income tax, (2) state income tax, (3) sales tax, franchise and excise tax, and (4) payroll tax.
3. *Stock exchange reports.* If the stock of a corporation is listed on one of the stock exchanges certain statements must be filed on a regular basis with the individual exchange.
4. *Reports to regulatory commissions.* Those commissions to which reports must be made under prescribed conditions include the Federal Power Commission, the Interstate Commerce Commission, and the Federal Communications Commission.
5. *Reports to the Securities and Exchange Commission.* Corporations that wish to offer a security issue to the general public must file financial statements with the SEC. Those corporations with their securities listed on one of the stock exchanges (as well as other corporations not listed but that meet certain tests of size or ownership distribution) also must file financial statements with the SEC.
6. *Reports to financial institutions.* These reports would be designed to meet the requirements of the particular institution for the purposes of obtaining credit.
7. *Reports to credit rating agencies.* These reports are usually designed by the credit rating agency to gain specific information from firms for credit rating purposes.

Excerpts from the 1976 Annual Report of The Monarch Machine Tool Company are presented as an example of financial statements prepared by corporate management for external users (Exhibit 6-1).

**Exhibit 6-1
The Monarch Machine Tool Annual Report, 1976**

President's Report

Monarch earnings for 1976 were $4,662,175, or $5.38 per common share. This return was 15.65 percent on shareholder equity and 6.7 percent on sales for the year. Shareholder equity increased by 10.8 percent to $33,016,162.

Sales were down from the record level of 1975. This was due to lower volume in strip processing machinery, particularly at our plant in France.

Higher earnings, despite the decline in sales, were primarily attributable to improvements in our U.S. machine tool operations. We also accomplished a turnaround in our combined European operations from a loss in 1975 to a profit in 1976.

Dividends per common share totalled $1.50, including regular quarterly payments of $0.30 and an extra payment of $0.30 on March 1, 1976. Monarch has now paid quarterly dividends without interruption for 64 years.

Labor relations

On February 16, 1977 a new three-year contract ended a 16-month strike at our Stamco division in New Bremen, Ohio. Also, a two-year wage settlement at our plant in Cortland, New York was signed on October 4, 1976.

Unfortunately, however, a strike called by the International Association of Machinists and Aerospace Workers at our Sidney, Ohio plant on November 29, 1976 continues as of the date of this message.

In recent years, there has been continuing deterioration in the labor climate in Ohio's Miami Valley where our Sidney and New Bremen plants are located. There is a shortage of skilled labor, to which Monarch and other local employers have responded with intensive recruiting and training programs. Monarch has also contributed to a new vocational school in the area. Unfortunately, these constructive efforts have been severely undercut by negative attitudes and disruptive actions within the labor force.

Management will continue its best efforts to resolve the present situation, but only in a manner that will be equitable to all concerned. We cannot, for the sake of expediency, jeopardize the future. To prosper, the Company needs a favorable environment. We must have the freedom and flexibility to operate and maintain the productive capability of our plants in a way and at a cost that will enable us to react quickly to market conditions, to price our products at a salable level and to maintain a profitable operation. Any labor contract which does not permit this is self-defeating.

During the strike, our shop management, engineering, service and other personnel are fulfilling the service requirements of our customers. Additionally, we are assembling and shipping machines for which completed components and assemblies are on hand.

Note: The 1976 annual financial report of The Monarch Machine Tool Co. is reprinted with their permission.

Exhibit 6-1 (continued)

Operations

Decisions over the past decade to broaden our product lines and to establish manufacturing operations in both the United States and Europe have been beneficial to the Company. Sales and earnings have been enhanced, and we are now less vulnerable to adverse market conditions than when we produced a single product line in a single plant. While all of our present divisions and subsidiaries manufacture capital goods, there is nonetheless a balancing effect in having plants here and abroad serving different markets with different product lines.

In 1976, our greatest return was from U.S. machine tool manufacturing, which also holds our greatest potential. There has been an accelerating trend in industry to use of numerically controlled turning machines and machining centers of the types we build. Because they greatly improve productivity and work quality, more and more of these machines will be required to offset constantly rising labor, material and overhead costs.

Our largest plant, in Sidney, Ohio, was a major contributor to 1976 results but, following the decline in machine tool buying in 1975, did not start the year with sufficient backlog to fully exploit its capacity.

At our Cortland, New York operation, sales reached a new high in 1976, with commensurate earnings. For the past two years, production has exceeded the rated capacity of the plant.

Dean Smith & Grace, our machine tool subsidiary in England, also aided 1976 income. This company is our most significant overseas operation. It has opened the United Kingdom to NC machine tools developed by Monarch in the United States, and its foundry is providing high-quality castings for our U.S. plants.

In general, our strip processing machinery operations experienced difficulties in 1976. Stamco was on strike throughout the year. However, we were able to fill orders through subcontractors, thus avoiding irreparable harm to this division's marketing position. Earnings, as might be expected, suffered. In February, 1977, Charles R. Bradlee was named general manager of Stamco. His extensive background with major industrial companies equips him well for his new responsibilities. The plant has a good backlog of orders as it goes back on stream.

Comec had a low level of business in 1976. This followed a decline in Western European buying and the completion of a substantial volume of Russian and Eastern Bloc orders. With renewed marketing efforts directed toward a broad base, reasonable recovery is expected in 1977.

Stamco UK has made continuing progress since it was established, achieving its best year to date in 1976. This subsidiary serves principally the United Kingdom and Northern Europe but, together with Stamco in the U.S. and Comec in France, affords customers a choice of sources and currencies when buying our strip processing machinery.

Exhibit 6-1 (continued)

Monarch Werkzeugmaschinen GmbH, West Germany continued in 1976 to strengthen our marketing foothold in Europe for NC machines.

Marketing

Increasing use by industry of NC turning machines and NC machining centers has generated formidable competition, both domestic and foreign. In order to maintain a forefront position in the marketplace, we have intensified our research, development and marketing efforts on this class of equipment.

In September, 1976 we introduced at the International Machine Tool Show in Chicago four new machines which we consider to be the most productive of their kind. We also demonstrated equipment at smaller U.S. shows and in Sweden, Holland and England.

Looking ahead

Forecasts by the National Machine Tool Builders' Association and other industry sources are for a record dollar volume of machine tool orders in 1977. Our Cortland division will be able to fully capitalize upon this. Additionally, our strip processing machinery and European operations are expected to exceed their 1976 performance. On the negative side is the strike at Sidney. It has already been costly, but at this early date in the year, we cannot fully judge its impact.

In general, I am optimistic about the future of our Company. Our financial position is sound. Our top management, as realigned in 1975, has proved its ability to work as a smooth and efficient team. Our plants are well equipped and being kept up to date as we go. Our product lines are excellent and well suited to the needs of industry.

In due course, the actions we have taken to improve and expand the Company and the plans we have for further improvement will enable us to more fully capitalize upon our strengths. Our performance during 1976, following the 1975 decline in dollar volume of machine tool orders, is an indication of our potential.

Monarch management appreciates the continued support of its shareholders and will maintain its efforts to fully justify this support.

Kermit T. Kuck
President

February 21, 1977
Sidney, Ohio

Exhibit 6-1 (continued)

Management's evaluation

The year 1972 saw the beginning of a capital goods upturn, following a several-year decline in machine tool buying to a 14-year low in 1971. This upturn was essentially negated for Monarch by a six-month strike at our Sidney, Ohio operation. As a result of these conditions, sales and earnings suffered in 1971 and 1972.

Sales rebounded to a record high volume in 1973, but earnings were restrained by rapid cost inflation. In 1974, sales again reached a record level, and earnings, although improved, still were restricted by ongoing inflation and shortages of manpower and materials.

By 1975, operations were more compatible with the economic conditions and we were able to achieve earnings commensurate with a third consecutive new high in sales.

The efficiencies and momentum developed during 1975 enabled us to report increased earnings again in 1976, despite a decline in sales.

For more information see the President's Report on pages 2 and 3.

Five-year statistical summary

	1976	1975	1974 (1)	1973	1972
Sales, Earnings and Dividends					
Net sales	$70,079,598	$80,476,586	$61,049,539	$46,860,201	$27,126,205
Other income	472,815	355,500	395,854	367,698	422,874
Total	70,552,413	80,832,086	61,445,393	47,227,899	27,549,079
Earnings before income taxes	9,820,175	8,536,924	5,079,295	3,614,789	574,859
Earnings after income taxes	4,662,175	4,038,924	2,585,845	1,950,789	254,259
Earnings per common share	5.38	4.66	2.92	2.14	.05
Dividends paid (common)	1,232,580	898,887	649,732	446,691	326,531
Dividends per common share	1.50	1.10	.80	.55	.40
Percent net earnings to equity (a)	15.65	15.11	10.34	8.23	1.05
Financial Position					
Inventories	$23,360,349	$22,035,491	$23,258,398	$15,869,170	$11,347,499
Working capital	22,154,199	19,976,582	17,660,828	16,328,633	14,386,431
Shareholders' equity (net worth)	33,016,162	29,795,961	26,733,614	25,009,375	23,716,420
Equity per common share (b)	35.15	31.92	28.75	26.90	25.38
Shares outstanding, common (average)	821,770	815,870	812,165	812,161	816,621
Number of shareholders	3,803	4,096	4,121	3,815	3,920
Plant and Personnel					
Property, plant and equipment (net)	$10,551,810	$10,027,534	$ 9,648,680	$ 9,190,114	$ 9,564,819
Capital additions	1,678,385	1,449,928	1,553,464	721,498	1,016,726
Depreciation and amortization	1,154,109	1,071,074	1,067,276	1,067,492	989,629
Employment costs	19,184,005	21,266,033	15,693,736	11,937,824	8,881,445
Number of employees, year-end	1,803	2,021	1,260	1,169	956

(1) Reflects adoption of LIFO.
(a) Computed on the basis of equity at beginning of year.
(b) Based on the assumption that the preferred shares have been converted into an equal number of common shares.

Exhibit 6-1 (continued)

Price Range of Common Stock	1976		1975	
First quarter	23-3/4	16	15-3/8	9
Second quarter	24	20	20-3/4	15
Third quarter	24	20-5/8	21	17-7/8
Fourth quarter	24-1/2	20-7/8	19-1/8	16-7/8
Yearly range	24-1/2	16	21	9

Dividends		
First quarter	$0.60*	$0.25
Second quarter	0.30	0.25
Third quarter	0.30	0.30
Fourth quarter	0.30	0.30
Total	$1.50	$1.10

*Includes $0.30 extra dividend.
There is no principal market for the preferred shares, on which a quarterly dividend of 45 cents has been paid since issuance in 1968.
Common shares are traded NYSE. Symbol MMO.

Consolidated balance sheet

The Monarch Machine Tool Company and Subsidiaries, December 31, 1976 and 1975

	1976	1975
Assets		
Cash	$ 3,153,543	$ 2,102,332
Notes and accounts receivable including amounts earned and unbilled on partially completed contracts— $1,771,661 in 1976 and $1,624,000 in 1975	14,978,468	23,907,815
Inventories (Note 3)	23,360,349	22,035,491
Prepaid expenses	407,032	278,554
Current assets	41,899,392	48,324,192
Property, plant and equipment, net (Note 4)	10,551,810	10,027,534
Other assets	900,645	444,206
	$53,351,847	$58,795,932
Liabilities		
Accounts payable	$ 6,413,993	$ 7,075,771
Notes payable		3,194,603
Accrued liabilities	8,206,333	7,836,725
Advance payments on contracts	3,916,429	7,841,801
Accrued income taxes	1,208,438	2,398,710
Current liabilities	19,745,193	28,347,610
Note payable (Note 4) and minority interest	590,492	652,361

Exhibit 6-1 (continued)

Shareholders' Equity

Preferred stock (with value in liquidation of $4,699,520) (Note 5)	117,488	117,708
Common stock (Notes 5 and 6)	5,400,000	5,400,000
Earnings reinvested in the business	27,577,463	24,367,547
	33,094,951	29,885,255
Less common stock in treasury, at cost (Note 5)	78,789	89,294
	33,016,162	29,795,961
	$53,351,847	$58,795,932

The accompanying notes are an integral part of the financial statements.

Consolidated statement of income

for the years ended December 31, 1976 and 1975

	1976	1975
Revenues:		
Net sales	$70,079,598	$80,476,586
Other income	472,815	355,500
	70,552,413	80,832,086
Expenses:		
Cost of sales	51,738,507	61,253,030
Selling, general and administrative expenses	8,615,679	10,767,484
Interest	406,698	571,199
	60,760,884	72,591,713
Income before income taxes and minority interest	9,791,529	8,240,373
Income taxes:		
Current	4,782,000	4,650,000
Deferred	376,000	(152,000)
	5,158,000	4,498,000
Income before minority interest	4,633,529	3,742,373
Minority interest share of loss of consolidated subsidiaries	28,646	296,551
Net income	$ 4,662,175	$ 4,038,924
Net income per common share:		
Assuming no dilution	$5.38	$4.66
Assuming full dilution	$4.93	$4.30

The accompanying notes are an integral part of the financial statements.

Exhibit 6-1 (continued)

How the 1976 sales dollar was applied
Materials, supplies, etc.	$ .55
Employment costs	.27
Taxes	.09
Depreciation	.02
Paid to shareholders	.02
Reinvested in the business	.05

Consolidated statement of earnings reinvested in the business

for the years ended December 31, 1976 and 1975

	1976	1975
Earnings reinvested in the business at beginning of year	$24,367,547	$21,465,841
Net income	4,662,175	4,038,924
	29,029,722	25,504,765
Deduct cash dividends:		
Preferred ($1.80 per share in 1976 and 1975)	211,874	211,874
Common ($1.50 and $1.10 per share in 1976 and 1975, respectively)	1,232,580	898,887
	1,444,454	1,110,761
	27,585,268	24,394,004
Exercise of stock options and retirement of preferred stock	7,805	26,457
Earnings reinvested in business at end of year	$27,577,463	$24,367,547

Consolidated statement of changes in financial position

for the years ended December 31, 1976 and 1975

	1976	1975
Sources of working capital		
Net income	$4,662,175	$4,038,924
Minority interest	(28,646)	(296,551)
Provision for depreciation and amortization	1,154,109	1,071,074
Deferred tax credits	(460,000)	
Provided from operations	5,327,638	4,813,447
Uses of working capital		
Additions to property, plant and equipment	1,678,385	1,449,928
Dividends paid	1,444,454	1,110,761
Other, net	27,182	(62,996)
	3,150,021	2,497,693
Increase in working capital	$2,177,617	$2,315,754

Exhibit 6-1 (continued)

Changes in components of working capital

Current assets:		
Cash	$1,051,211	$ 319,857
Notes and accounts receivable	(8,929,347)	1,944,512
Inventories	1,324,858	(1,222,907)
Prepaid expenses	128,478	(269,996)
Net	(6,424,800)	771,466
Current liabilities:		
Accounts payable	(661,778)	(3,369,663)
Notes payable	(3,194,603)	(2,444,102)
Accrued liabilities	369,608	1,426,863
Advance payments on contracts	(3,925,372)	2,183,193
Accrued income taxes	(1,190,272)	659,421
Net	(8,602,417)	(1,544,288)
Increase in working capital	$2,177,617	$2,315,754

The accompanying notes are an integral part of the financial statements.

Notes to Consolidated Financial Statements

(1) ACCOUNTING POLICIES:
The following is a summary of significant accounting policies followed in the preparation of these financial statements. The policies conform to generally accepted accounting principles and have been consistently applied.

Principles of Consolidation. The consolidated financial statements include the accounts of the Company and all domestic and foreign subsidiaries. Significant intercompany accounts and transactions have been eliminated.

Foreign Currency Translation. In accordance with Statement No. 8 of the Financial Accounting Standards Board (FASB No. 8) current assets, except inventories, and liabilities of foreign subsidiaries are translated into U.S. dollars at rates of exchange in effect at the close of the respective periods. The remaining assets and liabilities are translated at appropriate historical rates. Income and expense accounts are translated at an average of exchange rates effective during the period except for inventories charged to cost of sales and depreciation and amortization, which are translated at historical rates. Exchange gains and losses are included in net income as incurred.

Reporting Income on Contracts. Where accurate estimates of costs are attainable, a percentage of completion method is used for significant contracts involving strip processing machinery sold primarily as complete production lines. Losses on contracts, if any, are recognized in the period they become evident. Revenues on all other products are recognized at the time of shipment.

Inventories. Inventories are stated at the lower of cost or market, with cost for substantially all domestic machine tool inventories determined under the last-in, first-out (LIFO) method. Cost of remaining inventories, including foreign, are determined on the first-in, first-out method.

Property and Depreciation. Property, plant and equipment are recorded at cost. Except for certain buildings, depreciation is computed principally under accelerated methods based on estimated useful lives. Upon disposal, the asset cost and related reserves are removed, and any gain or loss is recognized in income. Maintenance and repairs are charged to income as incurred.

Product-Related Costs. Costs of developing products and customer service costs are charged to expense as incurred.

Pensions. Pension costs are computed on the basis of accepted actuarial methods and include current service costs for all pension plans and amortization of prior service costs over periods up to thirty years. It is the Company's policy to fund pension costs accrued.

Earnings Per Share. Income per common share, assuming no dilution, is based upon the weighted average number of common shares outstanding and common share equivalents after giving effect to the preferred share dividend requirement. Income per common share, assuming full dilution, is based upon the shares as determined above, and gives effect to the conversion of the Company's preferred stock.

Income Taxes. Taxes are provided, at appropriate rates, for all items included in the income statement regardless of the period when such items are reported for tax purposes. Accrued liabilities include $1,365,127 in 1976 and $392,747 in 1975 of deferred taxes related to timing differences which are principally the United Kingdom stock relief proposal and the use of accelerated depreciation for tax purposes by one subsidiary. Other assets include $679,059 in 1976 and $54,953 in 1975 of deferred (prepaid) taxes due to timing differences which include the valuation of certain machine tool parts in LIFO inventory for tax purposes only. Investment tax credits are recognized in the year in which the credit arises. The effective tax rate for 1976 and 1975 is higher than normal due to losses of a foreign subsidiary having no current tax benefit and nondeductible foreign exchange losses.

No provision has been made for U.S. income taxes on the Company's portion of the foreign subsidiaries' undistributed earnings ($386,229) and the DISC corporation's earnings eligible for tax deferral ($593,479). It is the present intention of the Company to reinvest substantially all such earnings in foreign operations. Under existing laws a substantial part of any tax liability resulting from the distribution of earn-

Exhibit 6-1 (continued)

ings of foreign subsidiaries would be offset by available foreign tax credits.

(2) FOREIGN OPERATIONS:
The Company's interest in foreign subsidiaries located in common market countries is summarized as follows:

	1976	1975
Net assets	$4,235,050	$4,060,594
Net income (loss)	$ 174,456	$ (699,408)

Net sales include $19,453,417 in 1976 and $28,288,125 in 1975 of sales by foreign subsidiaries.
Net income (loss) of foreign subsidiaries reflects the effects of foreign currency translation for all accounts as required by FASB No. 8. As a result, an exchange gain of $636,402 has been recognized in 1976 and a loss of $180,897 in 1975. However, the translation of sales at current rates and inventories charged to cost of sales at the higher historic rates reduced income by $1,019,220 in 1976 and $32,094 in 1975.

(3) INVENTORIES:
Inventories are composed of the following:

	1976	1975
Machines in process	$ 4,550,238	$ 3,263,396
Parts, subassemblies and work in process	15,762,671	15,770,837
Raw material	3,047,440	3,001,258
	$23,360,349	$22,035,491

Inventories amounting to $12,191,200 at December 31, 1976, and $12,001,950 at December 31, 1975, are stated at last-in, first-out cost. Such inventories, if stated at first-in, first-out cost, would be approximately $3,184,574 and $2,477,760 greater, respectively.

(4) PROPERTY, PLANT AND EQUIPMENT:
Property, plant and equipment are summarized as follows:

	1976	1975
Land	$ 885,768	$ 885,768
Buildings	10,079,073	9,738,203
Machinery and equipment	17,994,843	16,665,051
	28,959,684	27,289,022
Accumulated depreciation and amortization	18,407,874	17,261,488
	$10,551,810	$10,027,534

Certain real estate collateralizes a mortgage loan ($514,014) repayable in monthly installments of $4,986, including interest, until 1989.

(5) CAPITAL STOCK:
Authorized capital stock at December 31, 1976, consists of the following:

Preferred stock, authorized 500,000 shares, $1.80 cumulative, convertible Series A, no par value, issued and outstanding 117,488 shares, $1 stated value per share.

Common stock, no par value, authorized 3,500,000 shares, issued 826,440 shares in 1976 and 1975 (including 4,500 and 5,100 in the treasury at December 31, 1976 and 1975, respectively).

Preferred shares outstanding are convertible at the option of the holder into an equal number of common shares; such conversion rate is subject to adjustment upon the payment of stock dividends and certain other stated transactions. The preferred shares are redeemable by the Company at $40 per share. Each preferred share is entitled to vote on the same basis as each common share.

In the event of liquidation, the holders of preferred shares outstanding would have a preferential right to receive $40 per share. The aggregate of such preferential amount is $4,582,032 in excess of the aggregate stated value ($117,488) of the preferred stock. The net assets of the Company at December 31, 1976, exceed the aggregate preferential amount by approximately $28,300,000. Common shares reserved for convertible preferred shares, stock options and an executive incentive plan aggregated 163,649 at December 31, 1976.

During 1976, the Company retired 220 shares of preferred stock, which resulted in decreases of Preferred Stock and Earnings Reinvested in the Business of $220 and $4,950, respectively.

Exercise of stock options resulted in decreases in Treasury Stock and Earnings Reinvested in the Business of $10,505 and $2,855 in 1976 and $160,641 and $26,457 in 1975, respectively.

(6) STOCK OPTIONS:
The 1973 Employee Stock Option Plan provides for the granting of qualified and/or nonqualified stock options up to a maximum of 50,000 common shares. Qualified options become exercisable one year from date of grant at 25 percent per year on a cumulative basis, and expire five years from date of grant. Nonqualified options may be granted on the same basis as qualified options, except at 85 percent of fair market value at date of grant. Nonqualified options expire ten years from date of grant.

During 1974 qualified options were granted to purchase 15,400 shares at $12.75 per share. No additional options have been granted during 1975 and 1976. Options to purchase 600 shares at $12.75 were exercised during 1976, and options to purchase 1,800 shares were cancelled in 1976. At December 31, 1976, options to purchase 13,000 shares were outstanding, of which options to purchase 6,200 shares were exercisable.

During 1975, options to purchase 9,175 shares under the 1966 Employee Stock Option Plan at $14.625 per share were exercised, which terminated the 1966 Plan.

(7) PENSIONS:
The Company has various pension plans covering substantially all of its domestic employees. Pension costs of $646,037 in 1976 and $495,267 in 1975 were charged to operations. The market value of pension fund assets and balance sheet accruals was less than the actuarially computed value of vested benefits by approximately $2,897,000 as of January 1, 1976. The 1976 pension costs have increased due to the Employee Retirement Income Security Act (ERISA).

(8) CONTINGENCIES:
In 1968, a Civil Action was filed against the Company in the U.S. District Court for alleged infringement of certain patents. In the opinion of management, the ultimate disposition of this matter will have no material adverse effect on the financial position of the Company at December 31, 1976.

The Company also has been named as a defendent in two product reliability lawsuits claiming substantial damages. Based on information available at this time and the advice of counsel, management believes that the Company should prevail in its defense of these actions and that the ultimate disposition will not have a material adverse effect on the Company.

(9) QUARTERLY FINANCIAL DATA, UNAUDITED:
The following is a summary of selected quarterly financial data for 1976:

	1st Quarter	2nd Quarter	3rd Quarter	4th Quarter
Net sales and other income	$16,068,538	$17,986,763	$19,001,482	$17,495,430
Cost of sales	11,721,604	12,936,814	14,721,300	12,358,789
Net income	887,974	1,078,838	1,161,219	1,534,144
Net income per common share:				
Assuming no dilution	$1.02	$1.24	$1.35	$1.77
Assuming full dilution	$ .95	$1.14	$1.24	$1.60

Exhibit 6-1 (continued)

Accountant's Report

To The Board of Directors
The Monarch Machine Tool Company

We have examined the consolidated balance sheets of The Monarch Machine Tool Company and Subsidiaries as of December 31, 1976 and 1975, and the related consolidated statements of income, earnings reinvested in the business, and changes in financial position for the years then ended. Our examinations were made in accordance with generally accepted auditing standards, and accordingly included such tests of the accounting records and such other auditing procedures as we considered necessary in the circumstances.

In our opinion, the financial statements referred to above present fairly the consolidated financial position of The Monarch Machine Tool Company and Subsidiaries as of December 31, 1976 and 1975, and the consolidated results of their operations and changes in their financial position for the years then ended, in conformity with generally accepted accounting principles applied on a consistent basis.

COOPERS & LYBRAND

3800 Carew Tower
Cincinnati, Ohio 45202
January 29, 1977

Directors and Officers

Board of Directors

Wayne B. Brewer, Chairman of the Board and President
Cooper Tire & Rubber Co., Inc., Findlay, Ohio

Charles M. Cole, Vice President
The Monarch Machine Tool Company

Lee D. Harmony, Retired, former Vice President
The Monarch Machine Tool Company

Kermit T. Kuck, President
The Monarch Machine Tool Company

David E. Lundeen, Vice President
The Monarch Machine Tool Company

Exhibit 6-1 (continued)

Robert B. Meeker, Senior Vice President and Group Executive
Hobart Corporation, Troy, Ohio
Tony Niemeyer, Group Vice President — Secretary
The Monarch Machine Tool Company
Donald E. Reichelderfer, Retired, former President
Armco Steel Corporation, Middletown, Ohio
John F. Torley, Chairman of the Board
Dayton Malleable Inc., Dayton, Ohio

Officers
Kermit T. Kuck, President
Charles M. Cole, Vice President — General Manager, Monarch Sidney
Nagle V. Gusching, Vice President
Louis F. Kritzer, Vice President
David E. Lundeen, Vice President — General Manager, Monarch Cortland
Tony Niemeyer, Group Vice President — Strip Processing Machinery, and Secretary
Robert M. Peters, Treasurer

Common Stock Transfer Agents
Citibank, N.A.
  Stock Transfer Department
111 Wall Street, New York, N.Y. 10015

National City Bank
  Stock Transfer Department
P.O. Box 5756, Cleveland, Ohio 44101

Registrar
The Bank of New York
  Scheduling and Special Projects Department
48 Wall Street, New York, N.Y. 10015

Monarch Divisions and Subsidiaries

Machine tools
Monarch Sidney, Sidney, Ohio. Division.
Monarch Cortland, Cortland, New York. Division.
Dean Smith & Grace Ltd., Keighley, Yorkshire, England. Subsidiary.
Monarch Werkzeugmaschinen GmbH, Hemsbach, West Germany. Sales and service subsidiary.

Strip processing machinery
Stamco, New Bremen, Ohio. Division.
Stamco UK Ltd., Walsall, Staffordshire, England. Subsidiary.
Coméc (Société de Constructions Méchaniques de Creil), Creil, France. Subsidiary.
Scen (Stamco-Comec Engineering), Paris, France. Engineering and sales subsidiary of Comec.
Comec Española, Madrid, Spain. Subsidiary of Comec.

Index

AAA (see American Accounting Association)
AACSB (see American Assembly of Collegiate Schools of Business)
Accountant's report (in annual report), 131
Accountants:
  demand for, 1
    projections, 2
    public accounting, 2
    women, 25-26
  supply, 1
    projections, 2
Accounting:
  history, 99
  literature, 89-104 (see also Literature in accounting)
  systems, 103-104
Accounting education:
  professional schools, 120
Accounting faculty:
  demand, 111
Accounting Research Bulletins (AICPA), 89-90
Accounting Research Studies (AICPA), 93-94
Accounting Series Releases (SEC), 92
Accounting Terminology Bulletins (AICPA), 89-90
Accounting Trends and Techniques (AICPA), 98
American Accounting Association, 105
  programs, 111-12
  publications, 95-97
American Assembly of Collegiate Schools of Business, 1, 2
American Association of Attorney-Certified Public Accountants, 105
American Institute of CPAs, 14, 105
  Committee on Recruitment and Equal Opportunity, 24
  professional development, 112
  publications order form, 113-19
American Society of Women Accountants (ASWA), 105
American Woman's Society of CPAs (AWSCPA), 106
Arthur Andersen & Co., 13
Annual report:
  excerpts from sample, 121-132
  The Monarch Machine Tool Company, 121-132
  President's report, 122-24
APB Opinions, 90-91
Atlantic Richfield Company, 22
Attorney CPAs, 26
Auditing, 22
  engagement partner, 14
  literature, 94-95
  local CPA firm, 19
  manager, 14
  team, 14
Auditing Standards Executive Committee (AICPA), 95

Balance sheet (example), 126-27
Big Eight CPA firms, 13
Business Week, 13

Carey, John L., 26
CASB standards, 93
Certificate in Management Accounting Examination (see CMA examination)

CFA examination, 77
  application procedures, 88
  areas covered, 79-87
  candidate study program, 77-78
  competency standards, 78
  eligibility requirements, 87-88
Chartered Financial Analysts Examination (see CFA examination)
CMA examination, 54-75
  how to prepare for, 74
  sample questions, 55-75
  times given, 54-55
Code of Professional Ethics, 89
Cole, Charles M., 131
College Placement Annual, 7
Committee on Auditing Procedure (AICPA), 95
Controllership, 21
CPA attorneys, 26
CPA examination:
  accounting practice, 28
  accounting theory, 45
  auditing, 35
  business law, 40
  how to prepare for, 53
  information about, 27
  review courses, 54
  review manuals, 53-54
  sample questions, 28-53
  times given, 27
CPC Salary Survey, 20
Crum, William F., 8

Department of Defense Audit Agencies, 6
Department of Health, Education, and Welfare, 6
Doctor of Business Administration degree, 109
Doctor of Philosophy degree, 109
Doctoral candidates:
  supply, 110
Doctoral programs in accounting, 110
Doherty, William O., 26

Ellis, Loudell O., 25
Ernst and Ernst, 13
Ethics, 26, 82

FASB interpretations, 91-92
FASB statements, 91
FBI (see Federal Bureau of Investigation)
Federal Bureau of Investigation, 5
Federal Government Accountant's Association (FGAA), 106
Federal Power Commission, 6
Financial Accounting Foundation, 106
Financial Accounting Standards Advisory Council, 107
Financial Accounting Standards Board (FASB), 106-107
Footnotes to financial statements (example), 129-30
Fund accounting, 104

GAO (see U.S. General Accounting Office)
Gerhardt, Paul L., 8, 110

Haskins and Sells, 13
HEW (see Department of Health, Education, and Welfare)

133

In-charge accountant, 15
Income statement (example), 127-28
Internal Revenue Service, 4
  Special Enrollment Exam, 75
    how to prepare for, 76-77
    sample questions, 75-76
Investment Company Act of 1940, 108
IRS (see Internal Revenue Service)

Jobs in Accounting:
  black accountants, 24
  colleges and universities, 8
  Department of Defense Audit Agencies, 6
  FBI, 5
  federal government, 3
  FPC, 6
  GAO, 3
  HEW, 6
  industry, 20-23
  IRS, 4
  local CPA firm, 18-20
  minority groups, 24
  national CPA firm, 8
    typical first-year assignments, 10-12
  other federal agencies, 6
  SEC, 6
  state government, 7
  teaching, 7
  vocation schools, 7
  women, 24, 25-26
Journals in accounting, 97-98

Kuck, Kermit, 124

Literature in accounting, 89-104
  accounting history, 99-100
  Accounting Research Bulletins (AICPA), 89-90
  Accounting Research Studies (AICPA), 93-94
  Accounting Terminology Bulletins (AICPA), 89-90
  auditing, 94-95, 102-103
  CASB standards, 93
  cost and managerial, 101
  FASB interpretations, 91-92
  FASB statements, 91-92
  financial accounting theory, 100
  fund accounting, 104
  journals, 97-98
  offical, 89-93
  Opinions of the APB, 90-91
  ordering, 104
  quantitative methods, systems, computers, 103-104
  SEC *Accounting Series Releases*, 92
  Statements of the APB, 94
  Statements on Auditing Procedure (AICPA), 94-95
  Statements on Auditing Standards (AICPA), 95
  tax, 101-102
  texts and general references, 98-104
Lybrand, Ross Bros. & Montgomery, 13

Management advisory services, 18, 19
Management's evaluation (in annual report), 125
Master of Business Administration degree, 109
Master's programs in accounting, 109

Matoney, Joseph P., 26
Mitchell, Bert N., 24
Monarch Machine Tool Company, 121-132

National Association of Accountants (NAA), 55, 106
National Association of State Boards of Accountancy (NASBA), 28, 106
National Society of Public Accountants (NSPA), 106
Nolan, James, 5
Notes to financial statements (example), 129-30

Occupational Outlook Handbook, 7
Opinions of the APB, 90-91
Ordering publications, 104

Peat, Marwick, Mitchell & Co., 13
Ph.D., 109
Price Waterhouse & Co., 13
Professional development, 19, 112
Professional schools of accountancy, 120
Programming, 22
Public Utility Holding Company Act of 1935, 108

Quantitative methods, 103-104

Retained earnings statement (example), 128

Salaries for accountants:
  black accountants, 24
  college teaching, 8
  FBI, 5
  federal government, 3
  GAO, 4
  industry, 20
  IRS, 4
  national CPA firm, 10
  state government, 7
  teaching, 7
SEC (see Securities and Exchange Commission)
SEC *Accounting Series Releases*, 92
Securities Act of 1933, 107
Securities Exchange Act of 1934, 107, 108
Securities and Exchange Commission, 6, 107
Special Enrollment Exam (IRS), 75
State boards of accountancy, 28
Statement of changes in financial position (example), 128-29
Statements of the APB, 94
Statements on Auditing Procedure (AICPA), 94-95
Statements on Auditing Standards (AICPA), 95
Statements of Financial Accounting Standards (FASB), 91
Stone, Willard E., 110
Sweeney, Daniel L., 1, 2, 109
Systems, 103-104
Systems analysis, 21

Taxes:
  in national CPA firm, 15-17
Touche Ross & Co., 13

U.S. General Accounting Office, 3

Weston, Marilyn, 26
Writeup work, 19

Young, Arthur, & Co., 13